I AM THAT I AM
ALTA MAJOR

Shortcut To Alignment
and
Enlightenment

To David
a gift from my heart.
Archangel Michael.

Michael El Nour

Front Cover Art by Michael El Nour

Editor: Eric Wilson

Antahkaranah
Post Office Box 591
Desert Hot Springs, CA 92240
www.Antahkaranah.com

ISBN Number: 0-9655990-8-6

Printed in the United States of America

INTRODUCTION

This book is a complete guide to awareness and enlightenment. It contains all the information necessary to follow the path of Initiations, with success.
Although this publication is in keeping with the latest developments in the spiritual current of today, nonetheless, it is the basic teaching of the Tradition, a gift from the Great White Brotherhood to the students.

In complete association with the Planetary Hierachy, the Great White Brotherhood is the keeper of the wisdom/knowledge and the light on Earth

TO WHOM IS THIS BOOK ADDRESSED?

To all readers, apprentices or initiates.

ORIGINAL INFORMATION REGARDING:

• The true nature of Kundalini.
• The Alta Major Center and its role in the initiation process.
• A simple and fast method for evolving.
• The use of homeopathic remedies on the chakras.

The alignment method using the Alta Major center has not been released until now, it is considered a secret, and whoever discovers it, according to the Kabbalah, is called a King.

"Somewhere, in each of us, there is an Adam, in need of restoration, in exile from the Garden. The goal of Kabbalism is the restoration of divine man through the medium of mortal man. We are, so to speak, both the laboratory and the chemist who works there. All of this is to say that there is an intimate relationship between man and his spiritual counterpart; the mystery of this relationship is to be found in the Sephiroth. If one can learn how to connect the thread that hangs down from the Sephiroth with the thread of one's own being, if one can discover the opening at the base of the skull one may begin the work of the restoration.

"from the book Kabbalah, by Charles Ponce"

Other books by Michael El Nour

- Manifestation, Conversations with Archangel Michael –
  ISBN 0-9655990-3-5

  Manifestation is the story of Archangel Michael
  embodying on Planet Earth and sharing our human
  adventure. Through this unusual experience, Archangel
  Michael delivers the principles of manifestation of the
  GodSelf in the physical dimension.

- A Kiss For Lucifer – ISBN 0-9655990-7-8

  A Kiss For Lucifer reveals the truth about the hidden aspects
  of religions as well as the role of the Shadow in the
  evolution of human consciousness.

  This book presents the unknown function of Archangel
  Michael in human history and his relationship with the
  Dragon. It correlates sacred lineages of kings and
  presidents, emergence of a great monarch, satanic tradition,
  cult of the Goddess, Rennes-le-Château, and Lucifer.

  Is DNA the genetic blueprint of degenerated Reptilians in
  human disguise, or is it the manifestation of God's plan?
  In *A Kiss for Lucifer* all these elements converge in one
  burning focal point: The preservation and evolution of
  specific DNA.

Michael El Nour is available for workshops and lectures.
Please contact us through www.Antahkaranah.com

I AM THAT I AM
ALTA MAJOR
Shortcut to Alignment and Enlightenment

1

Activating and connecting the head chakras
Head centers and Alta Major
Alignment with the Alta Major

INTRODUCTION TO SPIRITUAL HOMEOPATHY
Modifying your health in order to purify your frequencies
Definition of sickness
Chakra Therapy

I REMEMBER, I AM

Moving one's self along the path of awareness and initiation is, above all, a state of mind. Whether the decision was made consciously or not, the individual knows, deep within himself, that his life cannot be limited merely to survival or to the pleasures of life, to the acquisition of material possessions or superficial relationships. The goal in life, surely, is to discover reality, not only as we see it filtered through the five senses, but in its entirety.

At some point in time, you felt the need and decided to make a commitment to dedicating your true self, your essence, to the evolution, enlightenment and reintegration of your Being into the Whole.

Those who are incarnated with this desire have few — if any — doubts about the reason for their travel on earth; nevertheless, the human veil of illusion, which is sometimes too heavy, the conditions of living, the family in which you decided to incarnate, are keeping you away from your goal for a period of time.

Then your internal Master tries to reveal himself, to make himself heard, in any way possible. He is asking you to remember your true identity, the exact reasons for your incarnation; he is urging you to remember your divine nature in order to offer you the opportunity to return to your original, divine state.

If you cannot hear the subtle messages of your Master, it is more than possible that he will move on to the next stage; he will put you into situations or face to face with people who are just 're-membrances', just triggers that are put in your path to activate

7

your subconscious mind. And finally, if you still do not become aware of the Master's call, very likely you will find yourself in difficult, even impossible situations, until your ears will finally be opened.

The diagram below is taken from the book *Satanic Ritual Abuse and Spirituality*. Here you will have an overview of the steps that are to be carried out in any healing process or spiritual evolution.

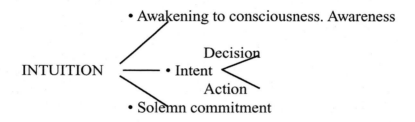

In fact, the day when you finally hear the call, an awakening to consciousness will take place within you. This is the point of departure for the Quest — an opening, a glimpse at infinity, a scent that will be enough to give you the strength to continue.

It is necessary, then, to make the decision to devote your life to your spiritual Reintegration and to act in accordance with this aspiration. The directions for you to take, the places for you to go to, the books for you to read will, of course, be presented to you. There are no miracles or coincidences, strictly speaking.

Your inner Being will provide the situations; it will make the books fall from the shelves or will send you the individuals who might help you evolve or change your life. Pay attention to the so called "chances" of life and consider them to be the interaction of your soul, your guardian angel, spiritual school and the like.

All throughout your life, but especially when you are already on the path to initiation, your Intuition will be your guide. If you are not in the habit of listening to its voice, then use your deep feelings, your guts. What do they tell you, what are your nervous plexuses doing when you arrive in an unknown place, in a spiritual group, when you meet a given individual? Do you feel at ease, happy, capable of using all your faculties? Or do your feel restricted, sad, anxious, dirty? Your body, one of the most precious tools at your disposal, reacts, speaks out, feels, and sends messages to your mind that are then left up to you to interpret — until you have fully connected all your spiritual systems.

Then, when you understand that you are on the Path, make a solemn commitment no longer to step aside; rather, you must resist the turmoil and pleasures that you will encounter, the weariness, the discomfort, the uneasiness, the doubt.

STRETCHING OUR CONSCIOUSNESS

Although any intent — in this present case it is writing — is and transmits an energy, this book essentially carries concepts related to the mind and the intellect. In order to bring about a change in your spiritual essence, you need to start using the tools that are already yours, that is to say, your mental abilities, your capacity for thought, within a physical body.

To give intellectual impulses to your mind means to store in your memories, voluntarily, a mass of information. The individual brings along with him a great deal of baggage. This baggage includes conscious knowledge and intuitive awareness — inherited from the past — of the blood that flows through your veins, the ability to feel emotions. In storing new and original data, you add this information to the culture you already have on a conscious level and to the sensations you experience. You are creating new combinations that will allow you to gradually remember the knowledge or facts that are stored within the maze of the conscious and the subconscious mind, in your atoms.

This process, combined with intuition, will create an expansion of your level of consciousness. Imagine a child or an animal whose universe is confined to the home or the cage where they live. The child receives information filtered through his senses, but this information is limited to the objects, persons and experiences he has access to in the restricted framework of his own home.

In the same way, although you are an adult, your understanding of the world and your behavior depend on the education you received, on the environment you grew up in, on the daily or intimate company you keep, on the more or less subtle development of your senses. Your faculties of perception, the way your body filters the information will shape the individual you ARE. As such, you act, think, love, and create a world — a world that is a reflection of your own vibratory frequency.

Our goal is to trigger the process of remembering, to cause certain pieces of information hidden inside you to rise to the surface, in order to STRETCH your LEVEL OF CONSCIOUSNESS, so that your reactions will be based on a broader range, on purified magnetic impulses.

As a first step, you are asked simply to let this message enter your brain, to expand your horizon, to see both larger and further.

Hidden within you, often in the form of codes, you have a great deal of knowledge — fantastic knowledge and capabilities. All you need now is the key that will give you access to all of these programs.

Our aim is to open up these programs that are a part of you, and then to help you increase your potential in an exponential way. We ask you to REMEMBER. *SOUVIENS-TOI.*

Any experience, conscious or not, is etched into your memories, into your DNA. But you do not know how to read, your DNA, your genetics, your past on a conscious level. For instance, the use of hypnosis allows you to recall to your conscious mind the moment of your birth. This experience, re-revealed, helps you clarify some of your emotional dilemmas.

Similarly, on a Universal scale, as a citizen of the Universe or as a galactic being, you can recall to your memory the moment of your entry into incarnation, or your appearance on the planet as a human being. This will allow you to know and clarify your feelings of Separation from the Whole, and to understand the reason for your terrestrial experience and your mission.

Thus we ask that you expand your intellectual limitations, using reading and then tools that will enlarge your universe, make you blossom, and change your perceptions of the world and finally modify your life.

The planet — and mankind — are at a crossroads. The vibration or frequency in which you have been bathed for thousands of years, is changing. Different magnetic impulses are striking your circuits. Another, more obvious change will take place in the atmosphere. Both physically and emotionally, you will have no choice but to be touched by these inter-planetary events.

It is now possible to work in the direction of this transformation, in order to prepare yourself to go through it naturally and not in shock.

All the more so, because the game is worth it; your level of consciousness and your field of action are expanding. You will have access to different potentials and various worlds. You are now being given the opportunity to recover the use of your mind — not of the fractional 10% that you already know, but rather all of it.

It is sufficient for you to go in search of your true self, in its entirety, to recognize your Soul.

REMEMBER. I AM THAT I AM.

To put yourself onto the path of initiation also means to recognize your universal citizenship, and then your place in the Spiritual Hierarchies. It is the spiritual family who is responsible for the existence and the evolution of the planet.

SECTION ONE:
WHO I AM IN MY PHYSICAL MANIFESTATION

1. THE BODIES

The human being was given the gift of a physical envelope, a glorious instrument, envied by numerous extra-terrestial species.

The physical body, at the same time it participates in the spiritual essence of the Hierarchies of the planet, is a vehicle to take you to extra-ordinary capabilities, often unknown and in any case unused.

To become aware of the body and its abilities is to grow, to place oneself in the macrocosm in a different way. Because — as a reflection of the whole of Creation, it is composed of atoms — the body has full citizenship in the universe, and the ability to communicate with its like in the field of the infinitesimal or the exponential.

In the heart of the atom there was laid down the spark of life — Divine life, the Light — that animates the world. The body, then, in its deeper and smaller structure, is linked to the Divine Creator and to the original Light.

The atoms, and then the elements, the cells, the organs and finally the systems, organized themselves for the edification of a whole, adapted to a moment in space and time — in this case, the human body, for planet earth, at a specific period in time.

The body, then, is the concretization of an equation of three hypotheses, which, with the addition of the Spirit, engender the Human Being, as you now know him:

- The atom or component of matter
- The place: the Universe, solar system, planet earth.
- The time: The temporal system, 5th race, 3rd dimension (for a very small amount of time).

Bodies — material life — are only the objective experience of Consciousness, the result of an interpretation of thoughts, which are filtered through the senses as well as one's education, both immediate and ancestral. Nevertheless, this envelope, as a part of the Whole, is a whole adapted to a very precise role. The Whole is limitless, infinite in time, space and quality, because it is the reservoir of the Spirit — Spirit itself. For this reason, the individual cannot be reduced to his visible or imaginary structures, accessible only to the material senses. The human being is not limited; he is restrained only by his vision, his awareness-consciousness, the image he has of himself and of his potential. Any Being that opens his consciousness will have access to other parts of him that are normally out of his reach.

The manifestation follows the law of the triangle:
1 is to replicate himself by bringing an impulse in 2, to engender 3. (Father-Sun-Spirit or Father-Mother-Child).

Man, in order to coincide with and reproduce the qualities of the Infinite, has a triple constitution. Finally, any Being, any manifestation exists on a system based on 7. For example, mankind evolves in a universe with 7 dimensions, with each dimension being divided into 7 sub-planes.

The seven planes of your cosmic system are:
- Physical plane
- The Astral/Emotional plane
- Mental/Manasic plane
- Intuition/Buddhic plane

- Spiritual/Atmic plane
- Monadic plane-Anapadake
- Divine plane-Adi.

The Monad, or pure divine essence, which comes from the divine realm, is individualized, then identified with a soul, and made denser, more compact, in order to cross the six next dimensions in its ascendant journey.

These 6 planes, then, are in turn divided into 3:
- Monadic plane
- Spiritual plane or plane of the soul (spiritual and intuitive)
- Plane of personality.
In its physical incarnation, the human being evolves through the personality or ego, which itself is triple in manifestation:

- Physical body
- Astral body
- Mental body

Each of these bodies has its owns atom or germ. They are called the physical, astral, and the mental germs. It is the merging of these 3 entities, in a harmonious motion, which makes possible, on higher planes, the development of the causal body. We have to discover these three germs in ourselves in order to make them manifest, to activate and synchronize them, and then to sanctify them. This is the work of initiation.

WHY THE INCARNATION

The body, in its triple manifestation, is the instrument that allows you to experience matter as well as the way back to God, the reintegration, through the progressive instillation of the Spirit. Because of his terrestrial envelope, the human being may evolve much faster than other galactic species or angels. The body is a participation in the Divine will to expand through the reflection of Oneself. It is this Divine act that triggered individualization, and the effect of Separation. These two conditions are indispensable in accessing Self Awareness, in the experiment of manifested energy.

Matter gives access to a multitude of situations based on friction, or energy expressed through opposites. These events
- project onto the individual an energy that leads to re-actions or changes. Physical plane.
- engender emotions modifying thought and the body. Emotional plane.
- generate a reflection, then an evolution of the spiritual Being. Mental plane.

PHYSICAL BODY

The physical body is adapted to planet Earth, which plays a precise role in the solar system:

1. This is the place where, in communication with the planetary Logos (the Lord of the Planet), we can learn the **Light of the Body.** The Light of the body or Light in matter is revealed by discovering Light in the darkness.

By the intimate awareness of birth and death, of production versus disintegration, we have the consciousness of the ultimate meaning of the opposites, the cycles, the law of duality. In matter, no one can live without dying; feeding one's self requires the phenomenon of digestion and putrefaction. The wound generates the renewal. The Phoenix is in all of us.

16

Considering our imperfect, sick body to be a temple, in which the Light, Divine presence or Shekinah is held prisoner, teaches us that only love, compassion, the gift, allows for the enlightenment of the Shadow in each of us to bring the Shadow progressively to the Light. Light springs out of the Shadow itself. In doing this, we participate, on our own scale, in the progressive enlightenment of the planet and race. We understand and accept the karma generated by the act of creation and accepted by the Co-Creators and planetary entities. Reconciled and conscious, we will broadcast a different frequency, one that has evolved, one that propels the entire race.

The mystic path, meditation, the discovery of I AM in ourselves, the revelation of the spiritual atom in matter, whatever the difficulty is, the apparent narrowness of the terrestrial vehicle, in situations and with Beings ruled by the darkness, are daily miracles that open up the path of the Divine within you.

The body is a densification that has a consciousness at a cellular level, a mind to think and a heart to be connected to God. It is organized with the densest part at the center — the bones — but it is also the spinal column that welcomes the purest energies and the Kundalini. This apparent contradiction teaches us the law of polarities, but it also teaches temperance and an acceptance of God's plan.

2. On planet Earth there is the symbolic Garden of Eden, in the middle of which grows the **Tree of the Knowledge of Good and Evil**. Although man no longer knows where to find it, Earth is one of the planets where the opportunity still exists to sharpen the consciousness by Awareness and to become God — or rediscover God (the Monadic plane and then the Divine plane). In the body the Being also experiences the ultimate love that is required:

- by participating in the divine experience of reflection and discovery of Self by means of creation.
- in accepting the karma generated by this event, as well as the karma of the planetary Logos.

3. On this planet an aspect of the plan of the spiritual Hierarchies is taking place for the Enlightenment of the souls and the restoration of the Light.

Here the important **question of supremacy** between the Light and the Darkness comes to be raised. A part of the creation made the decision to stay away from the Original Light. Some people call this the Luciferian rebellion. The planet Maldeck, for instance, was destroyed during a war between the white and the dark forces, indeed because its population was unable to find a balance and then reintegrate. The black forces are always on the lookout for a new opportunity to win the battle of the supremacy on any territory whatsoever.

You have an opportunity to be an active participant in this challenge, through the body. Take it!

The **physical body** lives in close contact with its double, **etherical envelope**, whose root is in the first chakras. The physical vehicle is fed by the sun, the light, the **Prana**, received and transmitted by the etherical body. The Prana, the principle of life, the solar fire, filtered through the coronal center, is integrated in its double aspect (polarities) and in accordance with the frequency of the spectrum. Prior to being distributed by the glandular system and the internal meridians, the energy enters the body at three points:
- Between the shoulders
- Above the solar plexus
- In the spleen

ASTRAL BODY

The **astral body** is an envelope of energy, hyper sensitive, an intermediary between the world of the form and the world of the spirit. Its energy is sustained by the astral planes of the body of the Logos, as well as by the Buddhic and monadic planes.

The astral body is made up of the sum of all thoughts and emotions that we have been emitting or receiving since we entered into incarnation. Therefore, it is possible to modify the make-up of the astral body by calming the most basic desires, working on quieting of the turmoil of our internal conflicts, balancing our emotional re-actions or changing our subconscious programs.

The astral body is connected to the subconscious mind, which acts like a kind of computer, without intelligence or without a spirit; it is something onto which data are recorded when there is a shock or strong feelings.

On the astral body are found the numerous energy hooks that bind us to other individuals, human or not, as well as organizations, groups, associations of thoughts — all of these determining a part of our karma.

The emotions, the expression of life, in an initial period controlled by the law of sexual attraction, must be understood and then transmuted to the vibration of the heart, the ray of Love/Wisdom.

MENTAL BODY

The mental unit has energy that is invigorated by the atmic, divine and mental cosmic planes. It corresponds to the inferior subplanes of the mental realm.

The mental or Manasic plane (from *manas*, "mind") contains the mental germ. It is this germ, implanted in the human mind, that allows a connection to be made with the spiritual planes. The mind is called the intermediary principle; it is the connection between the Spirit/Breath and the Shadow/Body.

Mastering the mental body means being able to control concrete and abstract thought. Several steps might occur:
- The ability to control ideas and projections that rise up out of the mind.
- In harmony with emotional stability, the ability to remain calm and put an end to our internal dialogue.
- The art of visualization that leads to the creation of thought forms.

Of course, the student's goal is not to be able to use 'powers' in a personal and selfish way, but rather to master the handling of energy in an ever subtler and more and more powerful way. This mastery will be dedicated to humanitarian service and to the Hierarchy, and will be a phase of the disciple's conscious integration into the loges of the Masters and Logoi. We must keep in mind that the Gods create and sustain the worlds through their Thought and Meditation.

CAUSAL BODY

The three permanent atom-germs - physical, astral and mental — come progressively into harmony, and then fuse. Energy is fire. These atom-germs belong to the Causal body or Soul Body. The latter is formed when the soul individualizes, through the contact of the energy of the Spirit and the Energy of Matter. Each causal unit, on the human plane, is the heart of the Monad; in the cosmic system, as a cell on the body of Logos. It is the organ of the expression of the Soul, which will function until the 4th initiation that marks the taking of control by the Monad.

The focal point of the Causal body is called the Egoic Lotus. Also named the Chalice, this center is formed by three ranges of petals that open little by little under the impulse of Consciousness and the purification of the different layers of the personality.

- Petals of Knowledge
- Petals of Love
- Petals of Sacrifice

Located in the heart of the lotus is the Divine Spark, the Soul, the secret revealed by the initiation.

* * *

The spiritual bodies, as generally understood, are, to use human language and understanding, made up of successive layers that are more and more refined and subtle. Their evolution depends upon:

- The development of Consciousness and then the ability to change your frequency in order to reach new planes of existence or dimensions.
- The evolution of the chakras and their organization. The simultaneous work of a group of chakras allows for the passage of new initiations, for a higher and more precise level of awareness.

Let us reiterate for greater clarity. A human being functions on temporary points of equilibrium. For example, life, actions, the frequency of X is based on the search for the ego, the understanding of one's personality in the world. X's general vibration, its center of gravity, is in this case, the 3rd chakra. As long as X works at vitalizing this center, connecting it to the first and second

21

chakra, a person's spiritual body will reflect the leader group 1-2-3. X cannot go beyond the 3rd dimension.

An individual who could develop the throat chakra to the point of making it more effective, who would then connect it to the second, has a spiritual body reflecting this mastery of the system.

As soon as you have understood and integrated the experiences, the frequencies inherent to a chakra and then to a group, you move on to another stage. Between the two, an initiation occurs, conscious to a given level. At the same time, the student runs across tools, teachers, books, groups or spiritual Masters, who will guide his steps to the next stage.   These initiations do not always take place on a physical level, but rather in spiritual dimensions, the student having attained enough mastery/consciousness of those planes, even if it is only sporadically.

Finally, although the body is a tool for reaching enlightenment, it is just a small part of your self. It is the center where your consciousness is temporarily located, but your Whole is still dispersed over different parts of the Universe, planes, dimensions.

You exist through the astral and spiritual bodies, and yet you are not aware of this. Therefore, it is easy to anticipate and understand the difficulty for a human being to be fully in contact with all the parts of the Self, all the dimensions and frequencies. Your true Whole Self is dispersed through other worlds, where heteroclite life forms are found. In addition to the creatures that are subtler than human beings, we catch sight of the species of the insects, the birds, the reptiles. For instance, parts of your selves, in affinity with other planets, like the Pleiades or Sirius, are at this moment invested in the affairs of your neighbors. It would then be important for you to develop the ability to travel to or at least to communicate with parallel dimensions.

The information and techniques offered in this book are tools that can open your consciousness and give you access to parallel worlds, as well as to your own multi-dimensions. Use your mind, train it every day by using your imagination, visualizing, and traveling with it. Increase your inner power, wake up your glandular system, the pineal gland in particular. Refine your ability to feel, so that you may consciously travel in other worlds and meet beings who have their origin in all the places in space-time, and merge with them whenever you wish to do so.

PRACTICAL EXERCISES

In order to prepare for the accelerated methods that will be given in the last few chapters, we are asking you, if you are not already doing so, to start a specific spiritual work and, as much as possible, to do it daily. The goal is to find an inner peace, to use the mind, to acquire the ability to see and work with the energies.

Choose a place in your home that will be your sacred temple, the place where you can withdraw into yourself, where you can meditate, pray, do your exercises. You will need a candle and a pillow or a chair. Arrange a vase, a plant, crystals — whatever makes you happy and seems to connect you to your spiritual practice.

At the beginning of any exercise or meditation, follow these steps:
- Be seated with a lighted candle in front of you.
- Clear your mind of any preoccupation — thoughts, people, worries.
- Breathe through your nose, calmly and deeply, 3 to 7 times.
- Each time you exhale, release your physical and emotional tensions; relax your body little by little.

23

Like the cosmos itself, spiritual techniques are dynamic/active and receptive/passive. For any period of inner searching, we recommend a balance between mental exercises and meditation.

By mental exercises, we mean visualization, projection, asking questions — to your Soul and your Guides. These techniques involve an active collaboration on the part of your brain, a voluntary act to lead your thought in a specific direction.

The visualization of the Light, of an energy, is the first step leading to a concrete understanding of subtle matter. You begin by imagining an energy or a flower, then you create the energy... and later on, the rose. If you think you see the energy, you will end up actually seeing it. Play at projecting yourself out of your body mentally, and then one day you really will visit India or the Mayas with accurate and verifiable information. Such results are possible more or less quickly, depending upon your previous incarnations, but the rate of attainment is increased through a daily practicing of life in and according to the Spirit.

Meditation is passive, it is a moment of silence. You are not doing anything, not thinking. In withdrawing into yourself, you are meeting the the Source, God within yourself. When thoughts and images beset you, let them pass by you like clouds, your karma is purifying itself at the same time.

ACTIVATION. FEELING THE ENERGIES

These exercises are suggested for beginners. Increase the sensitivity of your hands through feeling the magnetic field in the people around you, the energy of your pets, plants, crystals. Feel and acknowledge, on your own body, the physical symptoms and emotions of others. Test your discoveries in order to give yourself confidence.

To reinforce the creative power of your mind, close your eyes and play with your imagination. Any thought is a force that you send out. Train yourself to send out precise, simple images instead of letting your mind wander. Any time you need something, start by visualizing it and then ask the Universe to provide. When you need to call a friend, forget the phone and do it mentally. Before starting anything, such as looking for a house, a car, a painting, shape your project in your mind. The spirit is the primary substance, the fuel of the future. Train yourself to work with it.

Use every opportunity to develop your intuition. Read the people you meet. Guess who is on the phone, who has sent you a letter, the profession of the people you meet or their children's names. However, do not try to read the future. To do so would mean placing limits on yourself — and there are several futures.

2. THE FOUR ELEMENTS

Your occult anatomy is based on the presence of and intricate connections within your cells of the four elements of terrestrial matter: Fire, Air, Water, Earth, into which you gradually add the Spirit.

Your elements originate in the materialization of the Essential Fire, the manifestation of the All In One, The Non-Created, The Un-Formed. The four substances come from the first element or Akasha, Space, "The Matrix of the Universe".

Although we may discuss the four elements as components of physical matter, let us nonetheless bear in mind that air, fire, water and earth are first and foremost spiritual principles — intangible entities, made progressively more dense and then materialized in the world of form.

To assimilate and balance the four elements in your body is to integrate the four realms of existence — vegetable, mineral, animal and human. These latter represent the frequencies that you have been assimilating and that are preparing you to be at one with the Planetary Logos, with a new form of existence.

AIR

Air, the element of breath, enables the individual to live in the atmosphere. It enables exchanges with the environment, the oxygenation of the cells and excretion through the skin. A being, coming into incarnation with a dominant air, expresses his need for maturation before assimilating the other elements. He stays partially in contact with the spirits or his spirit as it was before incarnating. This is a need to remember one's spiritual self, one's receptive capabilities, the feelings of one's soul, of her sweetness, talents that make contact with the soul, for example music.

Air connects the soul to the body through the act of breathing. The lungs, the seat of breathing and of immediate life, allow energy to circulate through the body. They include alveoli (air-cells) that open and close, as a sign of perpetual exchange and of the balance of inhaling/exhaling, life/death. To refuse to breathe is to reject the incarnation. Any inflammation of the lungs, of the pleura, shows an inability to fully accept your experience on earth. Tuberculosis and diseases of the lungs are a reaction of the body's inability to adapt to the terrestrial elements, to the bacteria; they are a desire to break off relationships with others. A cold, an asthma crisis are momentary disruptions.

The circulatory system carries the oxygen. It links the will to live with the supreme expression of life imprinted in the blood and the chakra of the heart. Love cannot be fully expressed unless one accepts the human condition. Without unconditional love one cannot become a Co-creator.

Love creates, on the human plane, through transmitting life and heredity, which are imprinted in the blood. The student must surrender to this law of life, consider the child as a blessing, honor him, in order to refine and learn the responsibility of the Creators.

The Gods were given the responsibility for creation; some of them accepted it, as well as the karma resulting from this act. They still sustain and feed their creation, keeping it within themselves. The creator and the creation will evolve together and share cycles and karma. In the same way, if we have taken charge of souls, in our family, then we have to understand the reasons and spiritual contracts that bind us to our children and carry them to the end.

The lungs are connected to the heart by the pulmonary artery; it is the link between material and spiritual creation, the means to generate - ourselves and the external work - by integrating the four elements.

The air element belongs to the primordial creation, the universe and the planets being suspended in the atmosphere. The lungs are the link between the earth and the invisible aura around the planets. The nose, the external organ of the breath, serves to smell and screen the particles coming into the body. It acts as an antenna and as an organ of touch.

FIRE

Fire is the principal element of life on earth. Connected to the Sun and to the spiritual Sun, fire holds the magma, it allows for evaporation and condensation; fire has the power to purify and to destroy anything that is no longer adapted to specific circumstances. Fire is the will to live in the present, it is the power of matter. Fire contains in itself the other elements in an incandescent state. Air is fire made fluid, water is liquefied fire, and the earth is solid fire. To welcome the fire element in one's self is to agree to go through all the stages of matter and then through purification.

Fire binds us to our sun, the driving force around which the solar system revolves. Paradoxically, it also prevents us from rejoining the other systems, because too much passion, too many animal and terrestrial vicissitudes might cause us to forget the soul and her deepest aspirations. Fire, the creating element, is Shiva who animates or annihilates, the power of fear, anger and destruction. To love the element fire is to love and mix with all the realms; the spirits live from air and fire; the spirit is fire, the flame on the brow. It is also the baptizing fire. Associated with sight, the element of fire connects with the frontal chakra and opens the door from the terrestrial cavern to spiritual vision. No one has access to this type of vision unless he went through fire, that is to say, the challenges of matter.

Fire is the constructing element of Kundalini.

Kundalini carries the essence, the signature of the four elements. The terrestrial components, minerals, represented in the bones and the spine, are the support on which Kundalini rests; water is the ability to move, to chang; air is the breath, the spirit instilled into us by the Creator God; fire is the will to connect oneself to matter, to become embodied.

The serpent Kundalini acts as a driving force enclosing the four basic components, which themselves contain all the chemicals elements, whether terrestrial or celestial, manifestations of spiritual lives. In addition to the terrestrial elements, Kundalini also carries the essence, the promise, the possibility to merge one's self with the celestial elements. This alchemy is made possible by the modification of the chakras and the progressive addition of the external elements, which come from spiritual dimensions.

Kundalini is the fire of action, the devouring fire of a soul fusing with the spiritual elements in order to recover her complexity, her origin, her achievement. The chakras are the doors, giving access to the information received by the self in spiritual dimensions/realms and by our brothers from neighboring planets and systems. The centers perceive frequencies, sounds, smells that make them turn upwards, develop, refine, and then direct the information to the cells, using the channels of the nervous system and the synapses.

Kundalini holds the information integrated on earth, combined with the spiritual energies and our inter-galactic genetic heritage. The elevation of Kundalini is an achievement, the end of a long purification of the channels of energy, the chakras, the glandular system. The vital force, the spirit are then in their full power: their potential is momentarily accessible and in harmony. The ancestral hearth is reanimated.

WATER

The water element is the most feminine. It is a symbol of the flood, of the fluctuating nature of the energies; it is also an image of nurturing matter, matter that gives and sustains life. It is nutritional milk after having been the placenta. The element water is connected to the sense of taste.

To be connected to the water element is to accept evolving through the flow of life, an acceptance of being nurtured in one's body and mind, after being been born. The feminine principle allows for the expression of a life transmitted by the male principle, and then, within the terrestrial framework, it provides physical and emotional food. On a subtle plane, a being cannot find equilibrium without the feminine, receptive, element, the enriched energy of creation.

One can experience the water element completely in accepting sexuality and procreation. Sexuality is an act of communication, but also of surrender, a will to relinquish the self, to accept the mystery of life, the transmission of one's flesh to another. Sexuality is a manifestation of love that propagates the spark of life, accepting the role of the vase, the receptor, the tool for a new creation, then giving and nurturing without asking for any award.

The water element is related to the blood, the fluids in the body. The fluids nourish and carry. They are the receptors of all the living components brought to the body by food and the breath. They also convey the energy and the innate programming of any individual.

Blood and fluids are the protectors, but, like the reproductive and sex organs, they are a means of communication. They carry information. When there is an intruder, the blood will bring the news to the lymphocytes and to the immune system. In addition, blood holds and transmits all the genetic data, the memory of a given lineage, the treasure of consciousness of the group, of its acquisitions over eons of time.

To go with the flow instead of fighting — the law of non-resistance — is to surrender to the desires of the soul: the soul that wants to maintain, through any means, this vehicle with which she made an agreement. Before incarnation, and as a leader, the soul commits to the Lords of Karma and the being, momentarily despiritualized, in order for the being to encounter the vibrations and challenges that will fortify him, make him grow, and then return. These agreements, generally unknown to the physical being, are the occult reason why some people find it difficult to change what we might call the destiny. No one can run counter to the soul or God within one's self. One who is always fighting, instead of allowing himself to be carried by the flow, might, in fact, defy his own soul. It is a fact that we encounter obstacles that we find unbearable, because we are still wearing the clothes of human emotions.

Nevertheless, to the degree that we trust our own soul, where we make it a habit to listen to her, we will demonstrate our faith and the soul will make our path easier. This does not mean that the soul will satisfy our mere whims and human desires, connected to our incarnation and emotions. It means offering us a path on which to pass through this initiation called life.

A disturbance of the water element will weaken the immune system, cause problems of regeneration, as well as sexual and fertility problems. This person will have a nutritional dysfunction, relationships between mother and child will become strained; in fact, this person will have a hard time living her life to the fullest.

EARTH

The earth element is the consolidation, the unification with the planetary energies. Integrating this element means to be able to ground oneself, to be voluntarily anchored and connected to the life system on earth. It means recognizing one's belonging, at least for a time, to human existence; it means consciously participating in life and the evolution of the mother-planet. Assimilating the earth element means understanding the on-going interchange with the planet, which feeds humankind while they demonstrate their love and respect. It also means recognizing the bonding of energy between the earth and the other planets of the solar system.

To accept the earth element within the self is to become aware of the energies of the volcanoes and mountains, to take part to the phenomena that accompanied the birth and development of the planet. Through this evolution, through the maturation and reactions of the planetary entity, we are all growing and participating in the four realms; we are ready for another dimension.

The planet earth was chosen as a recipient for human nature; she sustains and guides the souls who have accepted the crusade of Separation and Matter. To go through human life is an honor of which we must become aware, because, when man is perfect, when he has returned to his Dvineness, he will carry, in harmony with himself, both the energies of earth and heaven. Through this he reaches a higher understanding, for example, than the angels. In return, the human being must experience this incarnation completely and in harmony with the terrestrial principles.

The earth gives us the strength we need to handle the ordeals of materialization. This powerful, magnificent energy allows human beings to live in perfect health and in harmony with the other creatures, to engage in the belief system that is the base of creation and life on the planet.

People who have difficulties on earth, who cannot create for themselves a harmonious and abundant life, are usually like uprooted trees, unable to communicate with their own environment. No tree can live from water and air alone. It must seek out, then accept and deepen its own roots.

Complete materialization involves the acceptance of the shadow sides of the earth, the entrails, the subconscious mind, the internal occult parts of the incarnated nature. These entrails exist, they have a raison d'être, and we must all participate in this initiation through the awareness of our own shadow.

Matter cannot exist without its entropic side. The challenge consists in experiencing the initiation of matter, with alienation but also with the pleasures inherent in this state, without the attachment that would prevent us from spiritualizing ourselves once again. After having been in communion, having understood and loved matter, we must pick ourselves up once again and be ready for spiritual reintegration. Paradoxically, the earth is associated with our sense of smell, odors being connected to the typically terrestrial cycle of nutrition/decomposition.

Earth illnesses: The earth element is related to the bones, teeth, hair and nails, to the mineral system.

EXERCISE

This is a basic technique, connected to the comprehension of the four elements, or to a passage in the four realms as represented on planet earth. It is a conscious connecting of oneself to the earth entity, in order to anchor yourself, to communicate with her and receive her energy. This exercise will strengthen you, improve the quality of your relationship to life, anchor you in incarnation, and fortify the first chakra. It is a way to become more centered, balanced, grounded, and to control your illusions about the world and spirituality.

GROUNDING TECHNIQUE

- Be comfortably seated, your feet flat on the ground, your hands in your lap.

- Inhale three times, deeply, through your nose. Hold the air in for 3 to 5 seconds. Exhale each time completely.

- With your eyes closed, focus on the first chakra - a spot situated at the base of the spine, at the mid-section between the genitals and the rectum.

- Then imagine a rope, or a tree connecting this point to the center of the earth. You might visualize the rope as being silver or gold or made out of light; the tree might have branches or roots. Feel free to imagine or let the images come to you.

- Feel the earth's energy rising up along this link and entering you, coming into your whole body, up to the tips of your fingers, to your hair. Communicate with this energy.

- As a second step, and to increase the energy of the kidney, focus on the beginning of the kidney meridian, located on the soles of your feet, in the hollow spaces between the joints. In order to find this spot, which is often painful, put your toes in the flex position. You will visualize an opening of 1 inch in diameter, through which you will connect yourself with the center of the planet and receive her energy.

3. THE SYSTEM I BELONG TO
I AM PART OF THE BODY OF A PLANETARY ENTITY

In order to know yourself, to easily change your internal plan of action, it is necessary to become fully aware of the fact that you belong to a Whole — one that sustains you, but at the same time also has its own karma and is pursuing its own life. This entity, then, imposes its own cycles on you, and you feel this on an emotional, spiritual and physical level.

You are the cells of a gigantic being. You belong to the body of a spiritual entity that encompasses and nurtures you with its vibrations. As seen through your eyes, this being is extraordinary. Its state of consciousness and energy may strike you as being almost inaccessible. Just imagine how, say, your white blood cell no. 3,674,923 might feel as it prepares to confront a germ inside your little finger. This cell is doing what it must. It knows its duty and that you will be grateful to him for carring out his mission. But, does this white cell have the same capacities as your brain? Did this cell do its yoga this morning?

This is an approximate picture of your relationship to the entity that is your body. To make it easier, let's make it a "him" and call him Entos. Entos has his own way of functioning, under his own system of laws, to which he must submit in order to breathe, live, communicate, evolve.

Entos has chosen to reveal himself on a specific ray, let's say the cardiac ray. His own chakra system is perfectible, at his own level, and this is the work he must accomplish. Entos's existence is ruled by his karma, which involves different experiences and states of consciousness. He also evolves in synergy with other entities, in his own system.

As one of Entos's cells, your existence is subject to the energetic fluctuations of his world and his body. Basically you will be working on the same ray. Just to complicate things a bit, you might have chosen to work with Entos, on one of his chakras, for instance the 6th one. Thus you have to improve your cardiac vibration, assimilated into the mental plane, and at the same time you have to develop your intuition, which is the 6th center.

Although his development is "advanced" compared to yours, Entos still has conflicts to resolve — conflicts that are affecting your own life. Of course, you are not completely at the mercy of Entos's problems. Your white cells don't ask you for authorization before they attack your flu. In the same way, although you are living surrounded by the Entos's frequency, each day of your life can be a refreshing adventure and bring you a great deal of joy.

SPIRITUAL HIERARCHIES

A growing awareness creates an expanding universe and family for the self. The search for the inner god is, at the same time, both an interiorization and a huge opening out onto the outer world, to the Infinite, to That Which Has No Name.

How can you imagine that the search for the germ of the soul, buried in the deepest part of your being, might launch you out beyond the world and the galaxies? This is another evocative mystery of the duality.

You must, then, include the Spiritual Hierarchies in your journey. In this book, we will give a simple presentation so that you might orient yourself and remember that loneliness is just an illusion of your world, a state of mind. In the framework of your actual solar system, all Creation is propelling itself in an immense ascending move, one that pulls you along with it. From the spiritual realms, you also receive the blessings of those who have already completed part of the journey, several generations of cycles ago.

These beings, humans, extra-humans, Avatars, Masters, planetary Logoi, are there for you, to provide you with their blessings, to keep you in balance, in their amazing breathing and their meditation.

Sometimes it seems a bit difficult for a regular humanoid to reach them; nevertheless, there are invisible threads that connect all creation and, in particular, all those beings whose goal is the evolution of the self in the service of the Light.

In simple terms, let us say that, as small as you might be in contrast to these beings that are capable of holding and nurturing a planet, you are still part of their body. Thus they are aware of your presence and surround you with their Infinite and perfect Love, a force that supports you in passing on to you this vital fluid. It is then up to you to become aware of this phenomenon and to integrate yourself into it, to live it, to expand it. The arms are open — arms that you can feel, even if you still cannot see them.

The Hierarchies are organized in the manner of a pyramid. Above you there is someone who went a little bit further along this path; he will pass on to you the knowledge and energy he has already assimilated; this person in turn is himself assisted by someone who is a little more advanced, and so on.

Each one of you belongs to a specific family defined by a quality of vibration, in the same way that the Masters are the manifestation of this energy or ray. More precisely, you are connected to two different families. One is your terrestrial clan, whose ramifications are lateral, horizontal. The other is your spiritual group, whose organization is vertical.

The traditional literature reveals the existence of the Lord or King of the World, the Sanat Kumara. Originating from Venus, the Sanat Kumara, considered to be one of the "Seven Spirits before God," has taken a physical form. Obviously, his anatomy, whether or not we use this term, has nothing to do with that of a human body. Nevertheless, by his decision to become manifest, he has given a direction to all the inhabitants of the planet — whom he holds, sustains, and surrounds with his presence, his aura. He has also permitted a faster evolution of the entire race, by stimulating the seed of thought and the human being's faculty of discrimination.

The Sanat Kumara is assisted by three Buddhas of Activity, who focus on Earth the energies emanating from the head, the heart and the throat of the Lord of the World. These four powers incarnate the three main rays of action and are the source of the Will, revealed in the aspects of pure Will, Love and Intelligence. Three other powers or Kumaras distribute and regulate the energies that are now to be manifested on the planet. These 7 Kumaras form a body, working as a unit, and they constitute the 7 main chakras of the planetary Logos. They, in turn, are assisted by the Masters.

According to Alice Bailey, there are three groups who incarnate and distribute the three main rays, under the responsibility of a Master. These three entities are living in the Himalayas and are watchful to ensure that the offices under their charge are functioning well.

- The Master Manu is the prototype and guardian of the 5th race. It is up to him to lead political and governmental movements. He is also to ensure the development and the continuity of racial types and forms. His Energy, a manifestation of the ray of the Will, emanates from the head of the Sanat Kumara, and allows creation to find awareness through form.

- The Christ, Bodhisattva or world Teacher, is also known as Matreya. He represents Love and Compassion; his Energy emanates from Sanat Kumara's heart. Christ gives spirit to matter, so that, at the right time, form will be freed by the power of Spirit.

- Finally, the Mahachohan represents the aspect of Active Intelligence. He creates and reinforces cohesion between form and spirit. He is the source of the energy we call "electric" or creative fire. The Mahachohan works in correlation with the Sanat Kumara's throat chakra.

These three entities, then, represent the three aspects reflected in the creation, form, spirit and intellect, or, as they are manifested on the human plane, as body, spirit and Soul. In close cooperation with these three heads there are different Masters who support the disciples through the path of initiation. We can name Jupiter, El Morya, Koot Houmi, Djwal Khul, Jesus, Hilarion, Serapis, Saint Germain. Their functions are interchangeable and are not specifically known. People have different opinions about them, and we will choose only to say that they collaborate in the development of the 6th race, watching over the evolution of the spiritual stream, through religions and groups, but also as scientific research and art.

Changes have recently occurred in the distribution of the tasks in the Hierarchy of the planet. Since the information that we have personally received is incomplete, we will not give any more details here. See *Initiation, Human and Solar* - Alice A. Bailey

***

How can you consciously associate yourself with the Spiritual Hierarchies? Well, remember the three steps mentioned earlier. After the awakening of consciousness, you have to reveal your decision through your actions, and then you have to make the commitment to stay on the Path. If your heart sends the message of your Unconditional love and of your will to be working in close collaboration with the Masters of the Spiritual Hierarchies, they will hear you. Now, this doesn't mean that they'll come knocking at your door, either physically or in channeling; but they will open more widely the channel of energy between you and them, and they will create meetings or situations that will help you follow the path. When you are ready, you will be admitted into a spiritual class, at your level, which you will attend, at night, while you are asleep.

The strength and beauty of the frequency that you are broadcasting, the harmony of your etherical body, the progressive opening of the petals of the Lotus will all, without doubt, attract the eyes of those beings whose task it is to watch over the disciples and guide them on the Path to Initiation.

Of course, we are using the term Initiation in its pure sense. An initiation is a passage, a moment in time and space when your energies, prepared through continuous and sometimes compelling efforts, and supported by the planetary vibrations, will enter into harmony with the frequencies of the invisible Master. The communion of all these frequencies, then, produces in the disciple a sudden change in his intimate and spiritual configuration of energies. Generally, the student, unable to resist the beauty, strength and Light of the manifested Energies, will become aware that someting is happening. This moment of awareness is sometimes only felt on the mental human plane, but in general it is accompanied by psychic or spiritual phenomena revealing that the disciple has joined a different world. This impact of energy is also received by the chakras and the physical body whose molecular structure changes to a degree, more or less, depending upon the degree of initiation.

41

The veritable Initiation generates joy, an inner certainty of the truth of what has happened, a renewal of spiritual life, additional capabilities and knowledge and, finally, a closer contact with the Master.

One of the easiest ways to meet your spiritual family is to surrender to your Masters, at night, before going to sleep. Classes take place every night from 10:00 p.m. to 5:00 a.m. A good many people attend these classes, but then do not remember anything about them. However, this is the place where, freed from the prison of your body, you nurture yourself. This is how artists, physicists and writers find their inspiration and, the next morning, have brilliant ideas!

Always pay attention to your dreams, which, as soon as you start on the path, are often an emanation of your travels and encounters with Masters, spiritual or human creatures.

SECTION TWO: MY TOOLS

1. TRIANGLES

The universes, the solar system, the Earth are all built upon the principles of geometry. Included in your internal configuration are energy structures with geometric forms adapted to the dimension in which you are evolving. Most human being live consciously only in the 3rd dimension. The spiritual work you accomplish today is a preparation for the 4th and 5th dimensions (there is no point in speaking about further dimensions that are simply too far away from most of you).

The most simple shapes integrated in your structures are the square/cube, the triangle/pyramid, the circle and the spiral. The cube is a symbol of the potential inherent in matter; the triangle, that of the spirit. Flat surfaces, like the triangle, belong to the 3rd dimension; volumes belong to the 4th.

In this chapter, you will use your mind, and your intellect to develop your energy structures and bring them into balance in accordance with the law of triangles.

Why do we use the tri-angle?

At the beginning of time, "the One duplicated Himself. Inert matter (Akasha: the Primordial Mother) was touched by His Breath (Prana), and out of this union planets and humanities were born." Michel Coquet, *Les Chakras.*

The triangle is the symbol of the manifestation, the creation. You, as a human being, are the jewel of the physical expression of matter. Your system, then, is a reflection of the supreme movement that gave you life.

43

The human being functions according to a triple constitution: body - soul - spirit or physical body, astral/emotional body and mental/spiritual body.

Below is a list of symbols that you can connect to each other:

Body	Mind	Manas	Air/Breath	Eagle
Soul	Human soul	Buddhas	Water/Moon	Man/Angel
Spirit	Primordial Fire	Atma	Fire/Sun	Lion

In all traditions, we find the idea or symbol of the Trinity, in which:
> One is the Monad
> Two is the expression or reflection of the One
> Three is the creation, the result of fertilization.

In the Hebrew Kabbalah, Creation is represented by the three mother letters of the alphabet: Aleph, Mem and Shin — respectively, Air, Water and Fire. "The heavens were created out of the substance of Fire; the earth from Water; the Air from the Spirit, which mediates between the two." Wescott, *Sepher Yetsirah.*

You will not be surprised, then, to be asked to create triangles of forces in order to reveal, to give new life to the flows of energy in your body.

Interpretation varies about the way chakras operate, separately and together. In fact, any moment in time and space has its own quality, each of you has your own unique physiology, and your spiritual geometry is subordinated to the organization of your cells and to your vibratory frequency. Depending on the period you are going through in terms of initiation, several of your chakras are called upon to be working together, which means that you are creating a bridge, a synergy between two functions, in order to manifest a new vibration.

Let us go back to the beginning. The One, the Oneness, expresses, exteriorizes Himself and meets His own reflection. Then He is aware of and manifests the number Two. This is when the unique principle is able to move on to the plane of the triangle, which is the realization, the expression.

All traditions — Hinduism, Christianity, alchemy, astrology, etc. — convey the same concepts. We will mention briefly the Kabbalah. The Sephirotic Tree, this multi-dimensional tool, will be considered as a symbol of the primary search, of any student's basic work.

The tree has several meanings. Among other things, the tree is the discovery and the harmonization of the extremes in the self; it represents the will to live, to experience things, as well as the qualities or essences of the manifestation in their double expression - dualism. Here it is a matter of the awareness in the self and in the exterior world of the opposite/complementary polarities, in order to feel them, balance them and then go beyond them. For instance, disciples will find both beauty and ugliness in themselves; the disciple will identify both wisdom and foolishness in his behavior and thoughts; he will experience fear as well as a foolhardy confidence. All these experiences occur in the reality that we have created for ourselves, i.e., the kingdom of illusion, Malkuth in the Kabbalah. The student looks at and accepts as his own his creation, his weaknesses and strengths, until the illusion disappears to open the door to the perpetual and true creation, in the kingdom of the ineffable.

Little by little, the disciple builds a bridge between the opposing energies, which are then brought into harmony, into equilibrium. He will no longer go through extreme situations and feelings, through crises, but rather he will stand on the path of balance or the "middle path" represented by the middle pillar in the tree of life.

This almost intellectual understanding of the personality, the integration of the consequences and expressions of the duality, will affect the student's ability to re-act to his emotions. With humility and compassion toward himself and others, the disciple will be able to gaze at himself without cheating and slowly he will evolve. A pressure and then a harmonization will occur on the astral body, and then later on the spiritual layers. Please note the interaction of the 3 planes.

Concurrently, the student can exert a pressure on the path that physically materialize these emotions, and directly modify a vibrational structure. It is this that you aim for when your are doing your exercises on the energy level - meditation, visualization, controlled breathing, Tai Chi, etc.

As soon as the student reaches a harmony between two opposites on the mental and then the spiritual plane/level of existence, he creates specific ties between these two energy centers (from one energy center to the other). Duality is transcended, a new line of force appears between the two 'opposites', a manifestation of this recent comprehension, of the rediscovered oneness, the three of the triangle, Creation.

* * *

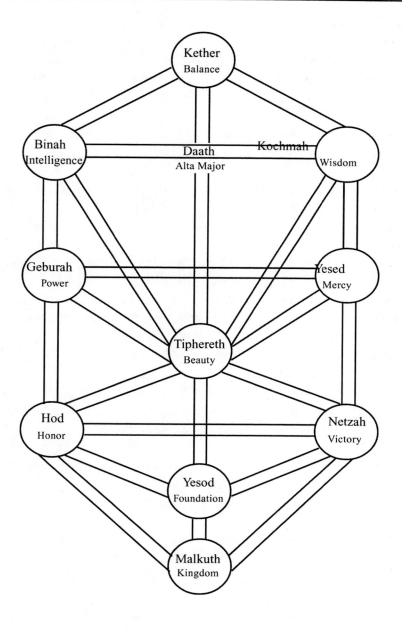

We suggest an alignment method, one that is both physical and spiritual. You have to create these lines of strength, of energy; you have to make your energies coexist in serenity so that, from within your inner self and having found your center, you will be in peace with the Universe and integrate yourself in it.

In conjunction with these visualization exercises, in which you will create these rays of energy, we must insist on two matters:

- Never neglect your inner purification, the creation of a strong personality, centered on loving will and not justify self-pity.
- Develop an acceptance of the self and of others, which is Unconditional Love.
- Any time your body lets you know that this is needed, you should have a session with a massage therapist, a chiropractor, an osteopath; cranial therapy is very appropriate. Here, too, you must use your intuition, your guts to choose a practitioner who is going to touch you, to change your energy circuits, by entering into your aura, into you.

Using the creative power of your mind, your will generate an interpenetration and a vitalization of all the centers. The bridges made out of ethereal matter, built between the chakras, prepare the path, facilitating the trajectory of the Serpent and, ultimately, your reintegration. No visualization, however, no mental work will ever be truly successful unless you have grasped the emotional and spiritual meaning of the process.

The techniques proposed in this book, then, are a basis for the work you will accomplish in your sanctuary, under the care of your guardian angel and the Masters of the Universe.

The first group of forces you are invited to concentrate on, which work in a tri-part way, deals with the power of matter. This is the basic work for any mutation of the energies. Let us repeat that it is not possible to have access to the highest initiations unless you have been through the terrestrial experiences and have integrated them.

The **lower triangle**, carrying the forces of matter, links the centers of the physical body. Connected are:
- The base of the spine. 1st chakra.
- The sex organs. 2nd chakra.
- The solar plexus. 3rd chakra.

This triangle represents the vital force inherited by any human being, the instinct of life and the faculties of reproduction. These energies are expressed in the need for self awareness and acceptance, often manifested on a primary level by adapting to society or the need for control.

The **higher triangle** symbolizes the spirit. The following centers are involved:

- Pineal gland.
- Pituitary gland.
- Thyroid.

The fire of the spirit is the basis for any expression. Life and form are created by the spirit. Consciousness is the presence of the spirit in form.

The disciple's goal is to become a living symbol of matter transcended by the spirit. This means that the Being must live and fully and deeply integrate his existence into [or: onto] the physical plane. The student understands the reasons for his life in the flesh; he participates — in his body, with his feet on the ground — in matter, truly assuming his human vocation. He relates to life without ambiguity, he is capable of working, nurturing himself, raising a family, all of this in happiness. A suicidal or anorectic temperament, for instance, shows a weakness of the first chakra, a physical or emotional inability to be connected to the terrestrial energies.

When this energy has been fully experienced, understood and assimilated on the conscious and unconscious levels, the student will no longer be dominated by instinct, by the subconscious mind, but rather by the spiritual forces in his head, ready to be activated and integrated on the cardiac mode.

The reproductive energy will have been transferred into the throat chakra for the spiritual expression of the self. This does not suggest simply and purely a rejection of sexual expression. The disciple must accept the natural experience of his body's needs and desires, without, however, giving them too much time or importance. Abstinence, which evokes restraint and effort, must be spontaneously replaced by a renewal of the frequencies and a natural transfer of the interest, the polarization of the forces, from the lower to the higher triangle.

A daily assessment of energies in a doctor's office reveals a disturbing propensity on the part of the disciples to disconnect themselves from their physical vehicle. The "aspirant" — the person aspiring — often goes through life with his "head in the clouds," neglecting his material or planetary responsibilities. This results in a physical and emotional dis-comfort, which will quickly disappear if you start consciously drawing upon the vast and powerful resources of Mother Earth.

Whatever your degree of understanding and evolution along the spiritual path might be, it is recommended that you ground your terrestrial energies more fully, that you strengthen yourself by practicing the technique below.

1. GROUNDING EXERCISE
See chapter 2, Four Elements

2. CENTER YOURSELF ON THE PINEAL GLAND
- Anchor yourself, as in exercise 1.

- Put one hand on the third eye, the other on the back of the head. Draw a mental line connecting these two spots.

- Then put your hands just above your ears and draw an imaginary line between them. Where these two imaginary lines intersect, then, this is the pineal gland, your center.

- Train yourself to feel and to visualize this spot, to balance yourself, right there, on your center, for at least 10 minutes.

3. BALANCE THE FORCES OF MATTER
- Be comfortably seated. Deep breathing, relaxation.

- Focus on the first chakra, at the base of the spine, and send light to this area.

- Then focus on the second center, which is located above the perineum, then on the solar chakra.

- After vitalizing and stabilizing these 3 spots, build a triangle of light between them; this will produce a harmonious synergy. Keep the image of the triangle for at least 10 minutes.

4. ACTIVATION OF THE CENTERS OF THE HEAD
- Lotus position. Deep breathing. Grounding.

- Focus in turn on the centers :
  - Pineal
  - Pituitary
  - Thyroid/throat

- Localize and feel the energy of these chakras.
- Vitalize them by sending them Light.
- Connect them with channels of light/energy. Keep this image in your mind for 10 minutes.
- Let go, breathe, give thanks.

2. LIFE PRINCIPLES

FOOD

It is not our aim to write a "how-to" manual, a list of absolute rules for you to adhere to. On the contrary, our purpose is to promote within you the realization that you are in constant communication with the God within you; therefore, you should feel free and able to make any decision without having to require outside help, and with the awareness that your choices are to be the ones most appropriate for you.

The same principle is to be applied with regard to food. Hundreds of books and methods have been published, promoting the best diet or the fastest way to get rid of excess pounds, to cure cancer or anorexia nervosa! Each of these formulas presents a partial truth and could serve you as a crutch at a given moment in your life.

We do wish to say, nevertheless, that most people have the ability to become healthier and their bodies to build fewer toxins and acids as soon as they begin to apply the principle of food combinations.

Proteins, meat, fish and eggs should be combined with greens and raw vegetables. The normal combination or proteins/carbohydrates is best avoided. In addition, a more efficient diet will also include proteins without fat. Carbohydrates, beans, pasta, potatoes and rice should also be combined with greens. Fruit should be served before meals, or, even better, eaten by itself and/or for breakfast.

This means that if you wish to re-educate your digestive system, you should eat grilled fish with salad and green beans, without fat but rather with lemon juice. At night you can enjoy some millet with vegetables, but not an omelet or cheese.

This type of diet — which is a bit hard to follow in daily life, especially if you have to eat out — should be a principle to be followed as often as possible.

If you have a serious health condition, deep-seated toxins, chronic eczema or indigestion, this type of diet will obviously make any medical treatment easier.

Quite logically, if the disciples simplify their diet, they will notice a corresponding change in their tastes. Natural foods — such as whole rice, vegetables, raw food, nuts — are the ones in harmony with the vibratory changes that occur during any period of spiritual growth.

Your ability to feel the energy of the foods you eat will lead you to adopt a diet of fresh and healthy nutrients. Vegetables, because of their contact with the ground, the sun and the light, are a gift from Mother Earth to humankind, a source of nutrition and a reservoir of energy. Frozen, chemical and canned foods do not recharge your vital energy, but merely pollute you, adding a further physical burden.

In fact, if you are sensible in listening to your body, it will tell you what is the appropriate terrestrial food. The law, this is even more than a principle, is to know what makes you happy physically and puts you in a stable emotional state — of course, we do not mean the ecstatic smile of the greedy person who has just finished off half a pound of ice cream! We also fully expect to hear some people claim that a long-term daily use of alcohol or marijuana makes them divinely ecstatic; we acknowledge their right to think like this or follow this belief if it is their choice or destiny, although we cannot agree with them here. Total realization and divine reintegration require a complete control of our afflictions and addictions.

Finally, some necessary words for those who advocate a vegetarian diet. It is rather obvious that refraining from eating meat, out of respect for life and in order to avoid ingesting animal vibrations, is desirable. Nevertheless, as long as you live under current conditions, and because of the physiological charges that take place along the path of initiation, each case is to be looked at and screened individually, with common sense, and including the parameters listed below:

- The individual physiological and cellular structure. Your constitution at birth and as later acquired.
- Life style, pollution.
- Spiritual development.

The act of eating has also been subject to the effects of pollution and the degradation of the human mind. It is true that any food might be presented in an agreeable manner, that a skillful combination of spices adds a secret flavor, enjoyable both to the palate and the soul. However, sophistication has been supplanted by the art of fast food, seasoned with chemical additives and treatments. You are probably no longer able to remember the smell and richness of a fresh piece of fruit or the flavor of home made bread.

And even if we cannot resist briefly pointing out these principles, nobody is asking you to take them literally or observe them daily.

FAITH

One of the fundamental challenges for the student on the path is the temptation to let himself lapse again, to give in when faced with difficulties.

Nowadays, because of the deep changes affecting our daily life as well as the planet, a number of you are suffering, often in silence, from difficult living conditions or the injustices committed all over the world. It is really a challenge to keep yourself on balance and to continue the quest. FAITH must be one of the foundations of your life.

Faith is the profound feeling that you have when you walk the tightrope stretched high above the emptiness of life; faith is the magical wild card that pushes you over toward the spiritual side. It is the thread that unexpectedly connects you to the invisible plane, the power of total confidence in yourself and in the Universe. You are not being asked to lay yourself open to danger for no reason at all, but rather, when push comes to shove, knowing that you can walk or operate in a dangerous area, is a manifestation of your faith in your own power to protect yourself, to become invisible or to know intuitively when it is time to leave.

To have faith is to participate intimately in any event, while it is happening, to experience it knowing that you are only going through whatever it is that your soul needs.

What we are talking about here is not just blind faith in a belief system, required by a church, a guru or even a god. All of these ask you to close your eyes, forget your intelligence and silence your intuition, so that you might consider them to be the sole authority, the only holders of the knowledge, the spirit or the energy that you need.

No, what we are asking of you is to have faith in YOURSELF, to identify and accept the Master, the God, the Guide, within you. The inner Master only provides the necessary information and energy, at the right time, the right speed, and modulates the intensity of the challenges that you can handle.

You must live according to one principle: YOU KNOW. It is obvious that not all of you are, at the moment, connected with your soul; therefore, you do not yet hear out loud the instructions that you might need. However, the game consists of changing your mental patterns in order to open up the channels of communication, little by little to cleanse the "static" and interference on the phone lines. And soon you will be able to hear more and more clearly, in all languages — i.e., body language, intuition, dreams, out of the body experiences, strange or fortuitous omens, meetings, the language of birds...

If, for example, you receive an advertisement about hypnosis or about the XYZ method of meditation three times in one week, this could just be an invitation to have a hypnosis session or to seriously consider meditation.

A cramp in your stomach each time you run into your close friend Paul or Peter, who just happens to be your wife's current tennis partner, might be an indication of a delicate situation.

A number of your problems will disappear as soon as you stop holding on to the solution that you consider to be ideal or magical. In order to show faith, the disciple must stop living through projecting his former self into the future, or the patterns that derive from his past experiences. Because, if he acts in such fashion, he cuts the way to any renewal or any change. In silencing your fear of the unknown, you are giving the Universe an opportunity, through your own soul, to perform a miracle for you. Do not forget that the Universe is infinite, omniscient and omnipotent. It would be a shame to reject such a partner. In order to be open to the infinite choices offered by the Universe, you have to live in and savor the moment, to find the good aspect of each and every situation, or the lesson that is going to make you wiser. Faith is an openness to the infinite potential of the Universe.

To have faith is to deny openly any attachment to fear. Fear is the emotional nourishment of the "dark side of the universe". To be attached to your fear, to live within anxiety, is to block any openness to the flow of divine energies and to the acquisition of a healthy and productive relationship to the light.

FEAR

Without any doubt, fear is one of your most dangerous but also one of your most subtle opponents.

Of course, you have all worked out your most obvious fears; you no longer have anxiety attacks in the dark, you can walk by yourself in the streets of New York, and you are able to walk along the metal railing high atop the Eiffel Tower. You even learned bungee jumping and you like parachuting.

Any apprehension that you have overcome was probably connected to memories of past lives that you have gotten rid of along the way. So far so good. But now you have to go much further. Even further, you say? Yes, you have to move on to fascinating, unbelievable new dimensions!

For the benefit of your own evolution, we ask you to banish any feeling of fear, insecurity, apprehension from your daily life. Thus, you will be free and will not slow down the creative processes of your mind. You will manifest openly what your heart desires and live in happiness and serenity; fully trusting, you will be persuaded that nothing negative can occur. Only those situations that you want to experience, to call forth, will be offered to you. Bear in mind that without ordeals or challenges, one does not progress. But if you live in harmony with your soul, having overcome fear, events are no longer catastrophes, or even problems for you; they are merely different situations, for renewed lessons and knowledge, and then expansion and maturation of your physical and spiritual expression.

— What circumstances and kinds of people make you feel uncomfortable? Who do they remind you of, what models from your childhood? When are you disconcerted?

— Why do not you dare to say what you are thinking in a situation of conflict? What is your relationship to these other people? Are they controlling you in one way or another? Do you need them, financially or emotionally, in order to complete a project, or to feel loved or desired?

— You want to move, travel, get a new job and yet you cannot make a decision. Why? What feeling is it that creates anguish for you, what is the situation that throws you off track?

— You know that your partner does not at all suit your needs; nevertheless, you are hanging onto a life that neither makes you happy nor is a credit to you. Do you panic at the idea of being alone? What is your real tie to your companion? Who is he/she replacing? Is it an absent parent? A friend? You?

Anything that holds you back from personal improvement, from change, any obstacle that prevents you from speaking out or taking action is simply FEAR.

You dread losing your job, objects, financial stability, the friendship or the esteem of someone else, a sexual partner. In a more subtle way, you are afraid of being found different, of facing an unknown territory or adventure; or you understand that the responsibilities inherent to your decisions are an encounter with your real self.

Any time you feel you are disobeying your own deep-seated personality, any time you lack integrity, that you feel some vague anguish, a shudder within you, then stop. Whatever the situation is, whether or not you feel fear, make it a habit to ask yourself this question: "Why did I do or say that is contrary to my real, innermost feelings? What am I afraid of? What, then, does this remind me of? When were other times that I felt the same way? Who was I with?

You will be amazed at your own answers. But you will be even more surprised when the day comes you change your attitude, your response to life.

EXAMPLE 1:

Let's imagine a situation that sends you into confusion. For instance, right in front of everybody, your mother, when angry, threatens never to speak to you again if you do not surrender to her will.

You have to wrap yourself into your cocoon in order to escape her zone of control. If it makes things any easier, you can isolate yourself physically by looking away and withdrawing into your inner self, breathing deeply and saying to yourself: "At this moment, I want to act as my Higher Self, I want to make use of all my abilities, and be my Soul."

You might possibly even fill your lungs and imagine yourself getting bigger, taking up more and more space, until you are Superman. Then, calmly, without anger, you can answer your mother: — "I understand your position and respect you. However, this is not in agreement with my innermost feelings or my point of view... "Your mother's anger will probably be appeased. While mentally sending her feelings of love and light, tell her: — "We will see each other next week, and I know that ..."

Of course, you will later think, "I was ready to stop respecting myself, to give up and let her control me." And then you will ask yourself: "What is the real basis of my fear? What situations from my childhood am I repeating? What is the real bond between my mother and myself? Is it love?

EXAMPLE 2:

You cannot put up with any more humiliation from the head of your department and you are afraid of losing your job.

Wait a moment for the storm to pass. Take a deep breath. Then ask yourself the usual questions: "Why do I accept the role of victim? Am I just repeating a program? What am I afraid of? Of raising my voice? Of being unable to defend myself? Of showing who I am? Of losing my job?...

Now can you feel this blessed state of consciousness that is yours during a deep meditation? You are quiet and relaxed, your mind is at peace, your body has let go, you are communicating with the divine, you have a feeling of expansion; deep inside, you feel strong, you are immune to any fear, any worries.

Choose the right time to speak with your manager, and tell him quietly that you deserve respect... If he takes this wrong, then that means you'll have to go out and find another job, for your own good.

CONTROL

Your entire system is based and organized on controlling relationships, where Love should be the key. You have been raised according to rules, to a precise code. These laws, this communal life assumes a structure based on the family, on groups, and then governments. It is clear that individuals get organized, help each other, gathering together according to common interests and goals. But is our modern society functioning on the basis of education and love — or on control and fear?

The family entity, the basis of society has actually developed in a context of fear. The tribal system began in order to give the individual a way to survive in a naturally hostile environment, and to ward off enemy assaults. In the 20th century, in the so-called civilized nations, people often hold on to their family because they are afraid of loosing a fellow traveler, so to speak, a means of support, a stable emotional space for their children.

The family structure is also built to reinforce the temporary domination of one sex over the other — either patriarchal or matriarchal. For the last few thousands of years, man has been the provider for the family, but also the one who holds the power; his presence has become necessary, at least in the minds of the family members, for the building and well-being of the family cell.
In order to create this situation, rules for interaction have been set up, principles that govern authority, the use of violence, the use of sex, the metaphysical belief system, such as: "Unto the woman he said, I will greatly multiply thy sorrow and thy

conception; in sorrow thou shalt bring forth children; and thy desire shall be to thy husband, and he shall rule over thee." Genesis 3,16.

On the individual level, because you do not know your place in the Universe, because you are uncertain about your beauty and greatness, you express your doubts, your own fear, through the need to control others. This pattern will manifest itself in your family life, your professional relationships, with those people you call your friends, your lovers. You want to know that these people belong to you, love you, agree with your system of beliefs, and act according to your principles and in your interest.

Please take a moment to reflect after reading each of the questions below:

— What was the real reason for the last "NO" that was said at your house?

— Why did you get married? Why do you jump up to answer the phone the minute you hear it ring? Why are you working or not working?

— How did you select your last employee, what "services" do you ask for in exchange for a salary?

— How do you choose your friends, who is the leader?

— Why are you working as a . . . ? What powers are you given because of this position?

— What are the principles of the church or religious group you belong to? Why do you love them?

— In your own mind, what is the value of money?

— Why are you not paying child support to your ex-spouse? Why do you wait for a phone call before you send the check?

— Why do you choose the music that your children listen to?

Let us talk about the way societies are organized. Prompted by a lack of individual consciousness — your neighbor might feel free to make himself at home on your property or to borrow your car- you have established laws. Originally erected in the spirit of protection, these laws set limits to your field of action. In fact, depending upon the country you live in or your family's religion, a pre-fabricated system of beliefs has been implanted in you, a system that is now controlling you.

These laws and principles are based on the fear of negative reactions from others, the fear, in fact, of being dominated or of losing control. But truly, how can one be protected from irresponsibility or madness?

Under the pretext of protection or belonging to a country or a nation, you have agreed to be controlled by governments. You know that they only tell you a small part of the truth about the real origin and use of money; they screen the discoveries made by science, forget to let you know that they have signed treaties with the dignitaries of some organizations or the representatives of other planets.

Throughout the centuries, the human race, dominated by invisible but powerful demi-gods, agreed to live in a context that limited it totally. Knowledge is confined to a very small part of the population, to priests or initiates. Without batting an eyelash, we admit that 90% of our mental faculties go unused. Society and especially the more esoteric religions still look with suspicion at any individual who has extra sensory perceptions and multi-dimensional abilities. A number of families and countries still do not question the authenticity of their religious books.

What would happen if one were to teach humans how to find their place in the Universe, to the point where they have a feeling of belonging to a body that will replace any need for law.

63

And what would happen if one were to give mankind access to the tools that promote osmosis, HARMONY, a natural consequence of the expansion and manifestation of UNIVERSAL LOVE. Who, then, would think about doing harm to his own body, about attacking the organ upon which his life depends? Well, suicide does exist, sometimes even among healthy people. Didn't our society simply decide to commit a kind of collective suicide of this gigantic body, mankind? Just how far have you been manipulated and by whom?

And what would happen if we were to teach children the laws of nature, respect and communication with plants, animals, the responsibilities inherent in any terrestrial citizen, love for the other, instead of having to educate them about competition and war.

And what would happen if, in the entire world, we would learn once again to listen to the language of the senses, to let one's guts speak, as well as intuition, dreams, the imagination, the poet, the crazy man... what is it to be a genius?

Restoration of the WHOLE human being depends upon the answer to these questions, the strength to live in real FREEDOM, the result of an awareness that promotes an absence of fear.

We ask you to feel, deep within you, to relive the reasons for this endless fall leading us to a dead end situation, to the degeneration of our bodies — chronic illnesses, cancer, AIDS — the degeneration of your children, of your beautiful planet. All together, let us integrate ourselves in the All in One; let us communicate, not on the basis of control, but rather on the basis of Love and CONSCIOUSNESS.

Consciousness can be taught, opened up. You are to participate in this process, teach your family and friends. Through your example and the specific vibration that you send out all around you, you will build or transmute the frequency of the planet. The way, then, is to enter the path of awareness, of the knowledge of your innermost self, and to modify your own basic programs.

COMPASSION/ACCEPTANCE

Remembering the intimate consciousness of your origin initiates and engenders your reintegration into the Whole. This Perception of your belonging to the universal consciousness erases and heals the feeling of Separation that is inherent in the human race. This discovery/perception of Unity, within yourself and with the supreme Consciousness, totally changes your belief system, your concept of events and other people.

As long as you are on the path, working on yourself, coming back to your center, your divinity might seem contradictory but is the mechanism to help you come closer, every day, to Unity.

Any actions and thoughts are interdependent, in both meanings of the word. If you suppress the thought, the attitude of Separation, then the feeling of isolation will disappear from your system.

The first result of understanding unity is to banish the old habit, the attitude of judgment. Any being that you come close to is right there in front of you, because, at any moment in infinity — whether it be recorded according to the notion of time as a period of 10 years or merely a single second — you are on the same frequency. It means that you share the same divine atom, revealed in a situation or a thought. This vibration is offered to you, visibly, made perceptible to your human personality, and looks out at you as if from a mirror. At this moment, open your eyes and your heart to understand what part of you is reflected in the other. Obviously, such a point of view is very helpful in order to regard others with compassion; not only is this reflection a part of you, but also, in the unparalleled love of the Unique Consciousness, it takes away the responsibility and the weight of anything that is adversely affecting you, anything obstructing your path, and then reveals it to you.

Compassion without judgment open the doors to total love. Mercy begins with ourselves. Whether or not you have already found God within you, appreciate the being that you are, open your eyes to find the revelation of your own beauty and greatness. Stop just thinking about those dreams or goals that you set for yourself as the only reference value. You must also appreciate the miracles that you have worked until now. When a child learns to walk, he already learned how to see, listen, babble. His body has been growing from a cell, and he has performed the feat of entering it with his soul! You are not yet a millionaire, but you have gone back to school, you paint like Picasso, you threw away your crutches, you are finally able to smile, you are experiencing extraordinary meditations, your health has improved a great deal, and all by yourself you have been taking care of four children, two cats and a dog!

There is only one Spirit, only one Universal Consciousness, that has revealed itself to the masses. You are but one aspect of this manifestation, a unique moment of the Source. Therefore, whatever your challenge might be, it is only a movement to lead you back to the center, the "reservoir' of the Spirit.

Judgment is a closure, the voluntary decision to set limits to your world and the possibility of expanding your awareness. Differences with others have to be looked at as paths on which to reach the Light. Tight, rigid laws and principles, if they are not an expression of your soul, are only the expressions of an education or of the group/system in which you are incarnated.

Acceptance is also the possibility to see the other, in his completeness, as a spiritual entity, as a Master even if he is hiding behind the thick cloak of a suffering human being. Exchange your ideas, reactions, methods. Honor the other in order to help him grow and for what he can bring to you, whether you see this clearly or not.

It is difficult to imagine, in the immediate future, a radical change in the governments and the laws, to such a point that they will be a reflection of the divine Consciousness. For the moment, then, you will have to adapt yourself to the system in which you are living, modifying your behavior on the intuition of the Divinity, which resides within your heart. Bear in mind that transformation, movement are natural, but fighting engenders resistance.

Purification or re-creation of the essence of each of you, individually, will generate a spontaneous change in the leading groups and laws of the planet.

More and more rapidly, old souls are remembering their origin and taking back their power. These souls show the fruits of this remembering, of this realization. Naturally, these beings are discovering their gifts as healers, psychics and artists, they are using energy and sound. They are forming study and meditation circles and are beginning to attract students on their own level of awareness. All over the world, in communities, these meditation groups meet regularly, harmonizing their energy through spiritual work performed together. In doing this, they are creating centers of energy that will transmit the message of the Light in a given town or country. All the vortexes initiated in the world will rejoin and participate in the metamorphosis of the planet and its magnetic field. These students, when they meet, also experience the sensation of completeness and joy, the internal peace created by the exchange and harmonization with others. This practice then motivates the individual who wishes to regain this state and expand it in time and space.

CHANNELING

After having sung all the vowel sounds one after the other, we decide to have a time for free toning: we first join hands and voices to chant some Oms together. Then each of us will express himself freely, toning whatever he feels. The results, harmonious or cacophonous, are sometimes stunning.

My chant and my energy suddenly merge with those of a participant. His voice has a beautiful tone, low and with a deep pitch, I am using my head voice. The energy becomes pure, lighter, and creates an door open to heaven. We rise up very high, as if we are climbing to the top of a huge cone. At the end, there is a temple of Light and Crystal. It is magnificent. A Being appears, majestic, his eyes filled with kindness, He descends, sending to us his Presence.

"Who are you?" I ask him.
"El Morya," he tells me.

I express my surprise, to which he replies: "The tunnel of energy you just created has allowed me to come down to you, into your own home. This is impossible if the vibrations are too dense."

El Morya comes closer and blesses us, putting his hand on my forehead. I have the sensation that a powerful wind is blowing around me, a light star shines on my third eye, tears are rolling down my cheeks, and I thank him.
The other participants saw a violet light; they felt the energy and an extreme peace.

68

* * *

Nowadays, channeling is in the mainstream of the spiritual search. For several years, especially in the United States, thousands of individuals have given their physical bodies, their emotional and mental abilities and sometimes even their lives, to spiritual entities, invisible beings who spread different types of information through channeling. The channels are supposed to receive messages and blessings from highly respected Masters, religious figures, angels, prestigious people who have passed away. At times, the communication is also established with inhabitants or messengers coming from other planets, neighboring galactic systems or parallel dimensions...

The channels and whoever is trying to receive energies and messages from the other side is then dealing with 4 different categories of individuals:
- Spiritual Masters
- Extra terrestrial beings
- Deceased human beings
- Angels and spiritual creatures.

1. The Spiritual Masters are Beings, who, either from Earth as part of the solar system or from other systems, successfully took up the challenges and initiations inherent in individualization and were able to regain their ties to the Source, in Consciousness and Co-Awareness, Co-Birth. These Ascended Masters rarely live in a body, although they sometimes use a physical manifestation. These Beings, in charge of Humankind, are relatively few in number, compared to humans.

2. Extra-terrestrials, as their names would suggest, come from neighboring planets whose destiny and evolution are linked to planet Earth. Their technology is without question far more

advanced than our own. Alliances have been entered into, and more or less respected, at an inter-galactic level, pertaining to their intervention in the human world. Treaties have been signed with governments that were eager to have access to their technology. In exchange, the extra-terrestrials agreed to respect human beings, to limit the number of abductions, experiments and their invasion of the planet. Extra-terrestrials master the etherical vision - not the spiritual one; they have access to desirable information that we have no knowledge of or that governements and religious leaders have decided to keep secret.

3. Deceased human beings also recollect data that were not available to them during their lifetime on earth. For example, they can look at their lives without any 'memory loss'. However, the fact that they are have left their physical body has not changed their general spiritual evolution and level of consciousness. The deceased thus have the ability to give interesting information about the other side, or they might try to protect you, but they are still not Masters. In addition, after a certain time, they actually do reincarnate and you might possibly contact part of your grandmother's soul or that of Napoleon, but not the person you dearly loved.

4. Spiritual entities have access to a different type of awareness and information than you do. But the entire range of vibrations exists in the cosmos, and the entities attracted to the channeling game are not the most evolved.

Some people say that they are in communication with angels or archangels. Once more, wisdom and good judgment are highly recommended.

Angels are a specific category of beings, in active service, who will answer if you call them. Let us keep in mind, however:

— There is a category of angels that are a part of you, a link between you and the Monad or origin. You just need to know yourself in order to merge with your angel.

— A human being, for the very reason that he has a body, has the ability to evolve faster than the angels.

We are grateful to all the beings of Light who take an active part in the spiritual awakening of the planet and its children. We thank them for the knowledge made available to human beings and for their protection, which is so often given.

Channeling, however, is neither an obligation nor a must for spiritual growth. We will even say that, for the student on the path, it is a dangerous and alienating activity. As a matter of fact, channels, subjugated by the knowledge or wisdom of invisible beings, forget to use their good judgment, they become the subordinates of the entity with whom they are working, they lose their own personality and slow down their personal evolution.

Finally, most of you have not clarified either your past or your body; you have still not met your Shadow; you do not know, for example, what percentage of shadow is in your intimate and genetic constitution. The people you attract like a magnet will always be a reflection of your own frequencies, your own light and inner battles at a given moment of time.

Like attracts like, as long as your subconscious mind has not been purified from all negative programming inherent in your childhood and past/parallel lives, you will continue to send out mixed vibrations that attract the same kinds of creatures.

The messages that you receive are also filtered through your level of consciousness and education. They are distorted by human karma, thought and vocabulary. Consequently, the channels who are capable of accurate communication with the Masters are rare indeed.

Very few disciples have spiritual vision. You must thus cultivate good judgment so that you might identify just who and what type of entities come to you. Instinct and intuition allow you to feel, within your body, in the pit of your stomach or deep in your heart, what kind of people you are dealing with. Finally, good judgment is the ability to see, to make a distinction, to make choices in using wisdom and the awareness you have already acquired. Keep your feet on the ground, do not let extra-human beings manipulate or fool you under the pretext that their level of scholarship or their psychic abilities are more developed than yours.

It is understandable that it is hard for you to turn down an opportunity to channel extra-ordinary information about the events that occur in the cosmos; the waging of inter-planetary wars that laid the foundations for terrestrial existence; the negotiations or councils now in progress to determine the future of the planet. It is pleasant and flattering to hear, on another dimension, that you are a spaceship commander, or that you are on a mission in a group or country. In this respect, there is one fact we would like to emphasize: special units have been sent by the Masters to carry out specific missions. But this does not mean that they have to interfere in our affairs forever. The channels, then, who pretend to receive communications from them might just be under the influences of different groups working for the dark side of the Universe.

It is natural to be willing to communicate with a supra-human entity who introduces himself as Jesus, Nostradamus or the Archangel Michael, especially if this will help you to create a spiritual group and be its leader.

Who can say with any certainty that he is channeling Merlin or Saint Francis of Assisi? And even if you were lucky enough or able to communicate with a Master, how do you know who is speaking with you? "You do not see but you *feel*" is your answer. How many among you are happy and emotionally stable to the point where you can use good judgment?

What is really happening? Who are these beings surging down upon the planet, using hundreds, even thousands of channels, in every home in Los Angeles and all the ships at sea — Los Angeles is a very suitable place for these kinds of phenomena!

Here we should make a preliminary remark. The fact that more and more people are developing psychic, telepathic or channeling talents fits in with the normal evolution of the race. In addition, you are also working on you own reintegration into the Whole. What does this mean? It means that you will be more and more aware of being part of a unique spiritual body whose divine energy, the heart, is located in and expresses itself through all creatures. Communication from aura to aura, from chakra to chakra, from whole to whole, is the normal kind of transmission of beings who have already spriritualized matter and made it sacred, who have already found and recognized themselves and reintegrated the primordial Source, which you are in the process of working on. All this explains your increased receptivity to the frequencies of the other side and your desire to use and acquaint yourself with this fascinating tool that you are discovering.

But, do planetary Masters, famous and powerful Angels, Archangels — we are not speaking about your guardian angels — have nothing more to do than to help the student on the path unable to make a decision or crying over his last failed love affair? Yes, you can connect with beings that are spiritually more advanced than you are, but not everybody has a direct line to Matreya or Saint Vincent de Paul. Also, as a result of the evolution of the spiritual Hierarchy, some Masters transferred their seat and left the planet for higher responsibilities. Thus they no longer communicate with the channels.

Entire books have been published whose content is supposed to be channeled information from the Masters. In reality, although the channels in question do receive their information from powerful entities, nevertheless they are still definitely working for the dark side of the Universe.

If one looks at a channel in using clairvoyance and spiritual vision, it is possible to say, first of all, if the recipient is pure and has consciously completed his redemption, and then chosen, with his soul, to work in the reconciled Light. Secondly, from the crown chakra, cords of etherical or astral matter connect the channel to one or several entities. These ties have a color, luminosity and structure that give information about the kind of entities one is working with. Finally, in following these etherical threads, the clairvoyant can reach the group of forces, the entity, or the group-form ["égrégore"] that projects itself through the channel; and even if it is difficult to name it specifically — after all, it's very crowded on that side! — at least will he be able to recognize it as working for either the Light or for Darkness.

We are using the word redemption to remind ourselves that all of us, especially the old souls, sometimes practiced the Art of the Darkness or were voluntary participants in certain gray brotherhoods in order to protect the Light. In addition, the conscious marriage of the energies, and thus the assimilation of the Darkness into our structures, is necessary to make the reintegration into the Conscious Light possible.

One final question. If you are a channel, are you really helping others to **become the free and evolved beings** that the planet needs? Or are you creating a new co-dependent link that destroys the intuition and growth capabilities of those people who listen to you? Do you have a tendency to create a group that acts like a cult?

For those of you who are consulting channels: was the information that you received on personal matters — such as your career, relationships, or spiritual evolution — accurate or did it just flatter your ego for a moment, reflecting the illusion you live in, or even the thoughts you are emitting, without helping you?

Let's take an example: the channel is a young woman, very pleasant, clear and reasonable. A whole group of friends goes to consult her, following the advice of Jim. Jim, who has already had several sessions with her, feels happy because the channel predicted that he would very soon have a brilliant future, that he would be successful in making money as a spiritual healer. Jim goes around boasting about the help he's getting from thousands of masters who are preparing him for the great task he has been assigned as a human being.

At the end of the session, we all know that we will have a new life, etc., etc. Weeks go by, Jim has organized his life according to these predictions and — nothing has happened; the dates were changed, but still nothing.

It is here that I decide to question the entities, supposedly angels coming from the 5th and 6th dimension:

"How do you explain that nothing happened for Jim?"
"He wasn't ready."
"You didn't know that he wasn't ready?"
To this, however, there is no answer.
I persist: "What do you have to say about his story — the one

where he was to have a great future, and thousands of entities to assist him?   Isn't one spiritual being of a reasonable strength enough to help one human being?" "Because he had no self-confidence, Jim needed to be flattered." "Oh?" I ask, in surprise.

Whoever it is that you are talking to, whether it is a human being or a creature pretending to assist you from dimension X or Y, always use your common sense as your best guide and frame or reference. First of all, the word dimension doesn't mean a thing if it is not located on a specific plane. If the answers given by the channels are not accurate, then ask them inscrutable questions and, if necessary, tell them flat-out what you are thinking and look to see their reaction. Does the entity respond to you with wisdom and love — or with anger?

Well known channels, whose writings have helped thousands of people on the spiritual path, have seen their nervous system deteriorate and their health become impaired. Their body could not handle the pressure imposed by the entities channeling through them. Don't you think that these extra-terrestrial beings, whether or not are they are working for the Light, should have had enough good judgment or love to avoid assaulting the channels and bringing them out of harmony? Doesn't this sound like a desire to satisfy a need for power, domination or human pleasures?

What the real spiritual Masters expect of you is that you rid yourself of all your terrestrial and human impediments and become an efficient tool capable of fulfilling your role in the cosmic scheme. You are then supposed to purify, refine your physical vehicle and establish the bridges between you and your divine soul, between you and the spiritual worlds. Once again, the first step is to free yourself from the emotional burden stemming from your past/parallel experiences, from the tendency to submit yourself to your outdated patterns and belief system. Through your reintegration and memory of the multiple aspects of your personalities, through the acquired consciousness of the self, you will have access to any knowledge you might need, to the archives and libraries of the universe, to these worlds orbiting the planet that you are aware of and that attract you.

The purification of your physical sheath will allow you to hear the voice of your soul, who knows everything. But in addition, your frequency will be so clear that your will be able to travel in other dimensions, to other worlds, and be able to explore and understand them directly.

Don't you think that this program is infinitely more exiting than the idea of meeting once a week with someone else who is supposed to be doing all that for you?

Make it a habit to believe in yourself, to rely on no one but yourself, and you will develop all your faculties, your intuition, spiritual vision, the memory of your past/parallel lives, as well as inter-planetary journeys. And you will be FREE.

A major COSMIC CONSPIRACY began thousands of years ago, one whose purpose was to change you, to cut off your natural access to the spiritual worlds and universal knowledge. Education, religion, gurus, the entire human system have all been contributing to your fall, lower and lower, because a group of leaders wanted you to be a silent and obedient animal, sometimes brilliant but limited because you are at the mercy of a diminished brain.

Let us be fair. At the beginning, this challenge was part of the application of a plan whose purpose is spiritualization and the evolution of the race. After the Separation, which forced souls into matter and form, the souls had to be given a framework in which any individual will have to, indeed will be forced to meet physicality in its more complete and sometimes even harder form. Among other things, this means clouding the awareness and vision that creatures had in order for them to fall into the realm of illusion, and then prohibit them from having any access to the spiritual dimensions. This was done by making the creatures unable to travel through all the dimensions as they had been accustomed to. This was the *sine qua non* condition of an intimate and full participation in the experiment conducted on planet Earth and in the karma of the planetary entity with whose body you are associated. This karma implies the necessity for any soul to know the two polarities that exist within creation, both the positive and the negative ones. The planetary Logos agreed to go through the "great sacrifice", to make the plunge that would take him far away from the spirit and into matter. As members, as cells of the body of this planetary Logos, you must participate fully in the sacrifice, i.e., the fall into matter.

The gods are not God. In constant evolution, they are subject to the laws of karma. Furthermore, the gods themselves are going through experimental and creative times, the results of which will affect creation. They can surrender to temptation, to the seduction induced by power, which will lead them to want to control their creation and lock it into extreme material limitations. This task was made easy by the original need to veil the eyes of the creatures.

Your responsibility is to understand what happened, and to refuse to be led back into a similar situation, regardless of the quality of the spiritual entities who contact you. Whether you feel tempted by a conventional church or a new age movement, do not let yourself be indoctrinated or dominated. You are a Master, you are God. You just have to remember and find the way that will lead you to this divine part within you. "And ye shall be as Gods, knowing good and evil." (Genesis 3,15). Does this remind you of something?

We would like to take a moment to consider with you a problem that more and more students are now facing, especially those who are working for the Light. Dozens of books have been published, often in English, that are the result of channeling. These books give you valuable information, especially with regard to the origin of the universe, the role of planet Earth and of us humans who are in the process of evolution of the races. Some of you have been expecting a landing of Extra Terrestrials offering to help humankind with technologies that you might need and new sources of energy. But how will you know who is really landing on Earth and what their intentions are? Just like your ancestors dating back to Biblical times, will you regard these space beings as Gods and accept their control with joy? More than ever, learn to feel, in your guts; develop your intuition and connection with the soul, in order to be able to hear the suggestions sent by your divine self, and increase your sense of discernment.

In a very simplified way, note the relationship between the Earth, Sirius and the Pleiades. Sirius is your Spiritual Sun. The Sanat Kumara has his head in Sirius and is an embodiment of one of the Rishis or Creators. The Pleiades are considered the wives of the Rishis. Thus, the seven Kumaras are balancing their energies with the Pleiades.

If spiritual creatures should contact you, first thank them for their presence, and then immediately state your intentions. A candle lighted right next to you, as a symbol of your commitment to the Light, tell the person you are talking to that you are light and work for the Light.

If you feel it necessary, state your desire to possibly collaborate with these beings, as long as they will not use your body without your permission, nor your energy to materialize themselves or participate to human life and sensual acts. Moreover, you will be

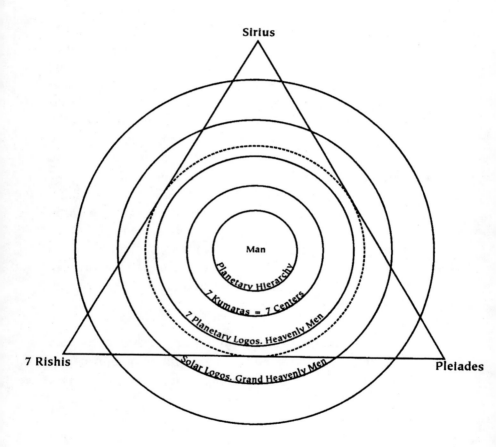

free, determined to use good judgment and wisdom to screen the information that you will be given. Finally, at any time you wish, you will be able to stop any further communications with these creatures who come to you.

In fact, whether you are interested in being a channel or not, do not limit yourself to any belief system you are given by someone else, human being or entity. But, in order to accelerate the vibrational change occurring in mankind, create a new life and system of communication, based on CONSCIOUSNESS. On the first level, consciousness is the intimate, innate sense of what is good or evil. For example, the instinct speaking inside you, in your guts, generally tells you that killing is not right. But, for some individuals or in different civilizations, in certain circumstances it is all right to kill.

What you are searching for, then, goes beyond education, culture or human limitations; it is universal consciousness. Through complete intellectual and emotional freedom, you will be able to approach Divine Consciousness, whose scale and strength are a reflection of the cosmos. If your world is limited to your family, your consciousness and potential level of consciousness will then be related to the territory, the space, the frequencies in which you are immersed. If your world is infinite, inter-galactic, based on a multitude of systems, beings, vibrations, openings, then your "judgment" will be infinite, your abilities expanded and coordinated on the different planes of existence.

Give yourself the means to reach this level of consciousness. Do not limit yourself in asking someone else what he knows or thinks. Look for awareness all by yourself. Like the universe, constantly in expansion/contraction, construction/destruction, use both phases. Go within yourself to find the Master within — which is meditation — and then expand yourself out into the infinite.

ABUNDANCE

Abundance is a state of being. It is the art of communicating with the reserves of the Universe, using magnetic vibrations. The key to abundance is giving. Give out love, send out vibrations of peace, beauty and harmony, and you will harvest gifts for yourself.

What is your definition of abundance? You would like to receive a profusion of — something, whatever it is.

Okay, most of you will probably answer in terms of money, although some people might wish for a large number of friends or ideas, a great deal of happiness... But let's take money as an example.

What is money supposed to bring to you? Any and all dreams are allowed: a car, a computer, more entertainment, freedom, joy, gifts for your friends, the end of stress, more self-esteem.

Before you continue reading, please take out a piece of paper and write down your honest answer to that question.

Well, whatever it is that you think money will bring you is generally the unconscious problem that actually keeps you *away* from abundance.

The solution? Work out this inner problem and money will come to you.

For instance, you think that a higher income will improve your self-image. Abundance is a part of love, with self love coming first. It is impossible to criticize yourself constantly and also attract the idea that you deserve most. Therefore, learn to love yourself; you will project a better image of yourself and will make more money.

82

Possessions: treat yourself to little gifts, allow yourself the right and pleasure to enjoy material things. Take away from your structures the habit of restricting yourself.

Freedom: Get rid of your personal barriers, system of beliefs, pre-fabricated restraints, intellectual limits. Free yourself and abundance will follow.

Home: redecorate, fix up and beautify your current home and learn to like it, for what it brings to you. This will change your own vibrations.
Stress: practice relaxation and meditation, heal the stress within you that is currently keeping money away.

In a word, search within yourself for the gifts you think money is supposed to bring you.

Now let's talk about the spirit. It is the spirit of abundance that dives down into the unlimited resources of the universe. You are the one who restricts yourself with the ideas your carry around with regard to yourself, to the world. You think that things cannot happen "rationally" in such or such a way, but human logic is not always the logic of the universe. Because of your concept of things, you are the one who slows down the cosmic answers.

First of all, learn to be part of the universe, like a cell in a body.

EXERCISES

1. I AM PART OF THE UNIVERSE :

    - Sit quietly and relax. Music is optional during this exercise.
    - With your eyes closed, you will stretch yourself to the outer reaches of the universe.

First of all, focus on the limits of your own body, your skin, and then the etherical envelope surrounding it, your aura.

- Visualize this egg of energy around yourself, about 2 to 4 inches wide. Feel this magnetic field, let your brain receive colors. Learn how to see, within your brain.

- Now imagine your magnetic field expanding up to 10 inches, 15 inches, 3 feet. What do you feel?

- Now, visualize just the opposite. Your aura is shrinking, it is now sticking right onto your skin. How do you feel? Well, this is a way to localize your aura.

Now that you have felt this energy, let it expand so that it touches the walls. What do you feel? A sensation of opening up, of floating? Don't stop yet. Go out of your home, leave the area, and travel as far as possible, on earth, in the solar system, among the stars. Can you hear the music of the spheres?

This greatness, this beauty, harmony in the machinery of the running of the planets must penetrate inside you and express itself in the kind of vibrations that you are sending out.

2. I VISUALIZE THE RESULTS INSTEAD OF THE MEANS

- Sitting, deep breathing, relaxation state.
- You are going to visualize the home of your dreams — not just the building, but also the way you want it. Make it come alive with the kind of people you want to have around you. Stage a play that brings you happiness.
- Visualize first the garden path, then the entry way. Remember to imagine, in color, the furniture, the interior decoration, the people, what is happening inside this house that makes you happy.

- Visit all the rooms, continuing to imagine your activities and interaction with the guests. As you do this, specifically spend time in feeling the emotions created by your interactions with others.

A word of advice: Do not insist on bringing in people from your past whom you believe to be indispensable to your happiness. Let your Soul and the Universe provide; they know what you need for a new future.

3. EXPRESSING A HIGHER QUALITY

This exercise will help you feel a type of emotion that you would like to bring into your life; that money, in fact, is supposed to bring you (Love, Joy, Self-Esteem).

- Sitting, relaxing, music optional.
- Think of this higher quality or emotion that you would like to add to your life.

What do you feel? Moved? Happy? Peaceful?
How does it feel in your body? Notice the changes in your posture, in your breathing.

- Now, imagine a scene, a situation in which you would like to feel or express this quality. Feel and bring this emotion toward you, several times.
- The scene is clear, enlightened, beautiful. Add even more light to it — and then feel it again.
If by chance you are just watching this play instead of participating in it, then now is the time to enter into it, to become a part of the play. Make the setting, the room more attractive. Sprinkle joy all around.

85

VIBRATIONAL POLLUTION

Most of you, for personal or material reasons, live in big cities. Such cities provide you with the challenges and interactions you need in order to grow on the path, but at the same time they can cause problems in terms of intense and sometimes harmful vibrational pollution.

All around you, people are stressed, physically sick, sad, even violent; but thanks to the discovery of different information and energy, you are encouraged to modify yourself mentally and in terms of vibrations.

You live in a period in which your sensitivity is refining itself and your chakras unfolding; as a result, you are more open to what other people are sending out, whether or not you are aware of the phenomenon; you must learn to test or see the energies of your neighbors, spouses, guests, in order to determine who they really are and what is really happening when you are with them..

Wherever you go and whoever you relate to, friends or gurus, use your inner sense of wisdom and listen to your gut feelings. If you have any doubt, physical discomfort or apprehension, please do not make any kind of commitment to these questionable individuals or groups.

* * *

You might have to be exposed to a certain quality of energy in order to modify your own, to open a path, to trigger a reaction or a memory. If this proves to be the case, you do not have to spend a long time with this foreign vibration.

This energy work can occur very quickly and the agent sent to you for this lesson will not necessarily be a master or a famous doctor.

The message might be sent to you through the last baby sitter you hired for your children, a friend of yours or even the mailman!

If you do meet a spiritual teacher, follow your progress, be grateful for this opportunity that you have recognized, but always remain your own master and keep your own power

EXCHANGES OF ENERGY

On a terrestrial level, the quality of your vital force depends upon your relationships with the people who share your different levels of existence. To make it easy to understand, let us speak first of all in human terms.

Your body of energy is very sensitive. It is your real means of communication. Any time you meet someone, an energy relationship begins between you and that other person, usually on the astral level. You perceive this tie being established, especially when powerful feelings are involved, such as love, hatred or sexual attraction. Something occurs to push you toward or away from the other. If you decide to or have to deal with this person — you want to make friends or you work in the same company — energy relationships are established. Threads of energy are being woven between your spiritual bodies, connecting the main areas of the whole being, physical body, chakras. You might imagine these links as being like a spider web, so subtle that you barely feel and see them when you walk cross your yard early in the morning.

If your personal bubble of energy, your etherical body is not yet very strong, the individuals that you meet will stick to it, depending of the kind of relationships you are establishing with them. For instance, if Paul perceives you as being very strong, he will have a tendency to try to draw your energy out, and will then connect with you in the hara.

87

Examples:

Laura thinks that you are sexually attractive and wants to plant a hook into your second chakra (genital area). As for Hector, your manager at work, he has decided to give you a hard time and has landed a tentacle in your solar plexus, next to the 3rd center. Well, we won't blame him if his aim was slightly off! What are you feeling? Paul drains you, just speaking with him on the phone is enough to wear you out or depress you, even if you do not especially dislike him.

In Laura's presence, although she is not your 'type', you find you have sexual feelings.

Working with Hector is a real nightmare, you develop cramps or get sick to your stomach!

What should your reaction to all these aggressions be? How can you maintain the integrity of your magnetic field, so that you may live and purify yourselves easier and faster?

BUILDING YOUR SPIRITUAL BODY

Your first assignment is to build your spiritual vehicle. You have to strengthen this envelope made out of etherical matter that bathes your physical body and is responsible of your balance, health and evolution.

In order to build yourself, you have to:

1. Know who you are, be fully aware of your strength and especially your weaknesses - nobody is going to cling, like a parasite, to a strong luminous area. What are your internal conflicts? Who has hurt you in this life? What were your relationships with your

parents, your family? Do you have a secret garden? If the answer is yes, do you also have the key to it? For example, your sister used to dominate you, put you down in public and treat you without any respect. Thus you now have a weakness in your relationships with older women, you have a tendency to give in, holding up your sense of family or duty as a pretext. How does your boss at work treat you?

2. Learn to recognize what is good for you, what gives you both energy and joy. This means becoming capable of saying no. No to all negative people, to all the situations that just aren't worth it - and we aren't talking about money here - and do not honor you.

3. Make a habit of talking out loud, saying out loud what it is that you want. This is a way to respect yourself and to ask others for their consideration. But you will also be using the verb form to consolidate your thoughts, to program your mind and announce your INTENT to change. This is the first step to success.

Let's go back to the example we gave you above. If your behavior, your response to Laura is clear, she will probably stop trying to make eyes at you or sink her hooks into you. But if your body language is ambiguous, she simply won't believe you.

If you expect your colleagues to respect you, but at the same time you show a lack of love and consideration for yourself, well, you can't expect them to treat you any differently.
A mother who thinks that her offspring has all the rights, because he is so small and adorable, cannot expect to be respected and in good shape after two hours with this little angel who is actually going to drain out all her energy.

Do not get into and/or stay in any situation that will damage or destroy your energy bodies.

If a power trip is going on between you and someone else, a karmic bond is being formed that will affect you not only on your physical or emotional state, but also the quality of your vibrations, and then induce consequences for your future.

IT IS YOUR RIGHT AND YOUR DUTY TO CHOOSE who you want to be, today and in the future that you are now building.

You are expected to act in an intelligent and responsible way, and define what links you want to build up, keep or destroy.

* * *

If you do not rid yourself of the energy hooks, you will soon look like a marionette, dangling from all these threads that give concrete expression to your encounters.

These links are what feed the people you deal with. One of them will be happy, drawing sexual or magnetic energy from the others. Another will find pleasure in controlling his brothers, a third person cannot exist without suffering.

These etherical connections and their originators are sometimes so powerful that they will remain on after physical death. This is the reason why you always meet the same characters life after life. Thus it is important, when you are aware of the process, to adopt a spiritual hygiene.

Do not let others decide what ties to them you want to keep or not. As soon as you meet someone, and especially if you feel any discomfort, solve the problem. TAKE CONTROL OF YOUR LIFE.

Of course, any action that is conscious and carried out physically or spiritually will create responsibilities. If a person who feeds

90

herself from your energy or conflicts is unable to live without this vibration, she will not want to have her supply cut off. This is the reason why we recommend that you state openly and out loud what it is that you want. If the human part cannot listen, use telepathy or light to reach the subconscious mind or the spiritual self of your aggressor. Then if this person cannot or does not want to hear, he will probably change his relationship with you. You will lose a friend or be sent to another company to work.

ASTRAL POLLUTION. ENTITIES

Finally, you must keep in mind that you live not only with other human beings but are also surrounded by spiritual entities. Although they might come from other dimensions, in actual fact, you share the same space.

These spiritual beings, according to their nature and level of awareness, are sometimes using you. They sense in you a potential energy, a mass of thought and emotions, a source of food.

If your frequency is refined and pure enough, an evolved spiritual being might visit you. But it is a fact that the creatures who are going to plant a hook into your astral body and vampirize you are not the ones you wish to have with you on a daily basis.

By way of hygiene and to keep your vital energy intact, it is thus advisable to have high-level thoughts, which will demonstrate your will to transcend your frequencies instead of being polluted. Whenever you feel sad or depressed, choose company that will nourish and vitalize you, understand your problems and solve them; use homeopathy or energy treatments, acupuncture, laying on of hands, ask for the presence of your guides.

EXERCISES

It is important to develop the habit of protecting yourself, in terms of energy; that way, while maintaining your sensitivity and manifesting your love for the other, you will not absorb things 'like a sponge' and you will protect the integrity of your subtle bodies.

1. Every day, during your 'retreat' into your temple, put yourself into your 'bubble of light'. In the morning, build columns of light in the corners of your room - or the place in which you meditate - and a fifth column in the center. Little by little, these columns will literally take form and will help you as a protection and a way of transmuting your energies.

2. Imagine your chakras as flowers that open toward the outside of your body. When you are in a difficult or unusual situation, one that you feel is wrong, visualize these flowers closing up for a moment.

For example, you might have the sensation that someone is trying to force his will or energy onto you. This pertains to the second and third chakra. Visualize, then, these two flowers closing up... and don't forget to open them again, you might be gifted enough to block yourself off for several days!

A friend is being too sexual with you, and you're not interested: close your second flower.

Someone is trying to read your mind... protect the sixth chakra.

3. Just as you shower every day to eliminate daily residue, it is advisable to shower with white Light if something or someone has disturbed you.

4. At night, in a sitting position or lying down, before you go to sleep:

- State the fact that you are going to cleanse yourself of energy pollution that has built up during the day.

- Think of the people you have met, dealt with, taken care of, and now visualize your ties to them as threads that bind you.

- Take back for yourself the energy that they have taken from you when you were with them, pull these threads toward yourself, and as you do this, feel the energy flow back into you, become integrated back into your own body.

- Then, while still keeping your eyes shut, give yourself time for people to come to you and present themselves to you. People whom you have not thought of and who have, intentionally or not, kept some of your energy. Or people to whom you have given the permission to take your energy or your life force. Take back all your energy.

- You will notice that your etheric body is swelling up almost like a balloon, to the point where you feel you are rising up in the air.

5. To break off your relations with an individual, see the chapter entitled Karma.

3. CHAKRAS AND KUNDALINI

"Tonight the women are meeting. We are all happy to be together. Sherry, my spiritual sister, Gabriella, a friend from the past, Maria, Laura... After helping the youngest to solve a problem, we are getting ready for a session of "drumming," of beating the drum... Everybody else is lying down, but I prefer the lotus position, with some item of clothing rolled under my spine, and without anything to support my back, which, for me, is a bit adventurous.

Sherry beats the drum with a steady beat. The sound is heavy and deep.

"You have the choice either of joining your Higher Self or your subconscious mind. For the subconscious mind, you might go, as deeply as possible, inside our mother, the Earth. For example , you can imagine yourself walking into a cave..."

Sherry stops speaking.

I immediately project myself into the womb of the Earth. Soon I am in a cave, lighted by a large vertical light. The center looks like a flame, almost white, extremely dense. All around there is a halo — shinny, moving, alive.

I go closer and hear:

"I am the Light, Nora".

I walk into the Light and merge with Myself.

As best I can, I have to stop my mind from saying to me: "Don't you see that you're not in perfect alignment?"

94

- "Okay, okay, I'll do what I can, but I just feel like surrendering. The drum beats regularly, and the sound penetrates me, deeply, in powerful pulsations. My insides are beating, and suddenly, the fire awakens. A brief tickling, and the Serpent Kundalini, almost like some kind of mechanism whose motor is beyond human comprehension, raises its head, with tremendous power. I follow it, see it, hear it, but I don't interfere. The Serpent passes by, almost without hesitation, along the two sides of my spine; distinctly I see Ida and Pinguala, different in color and composition. Then the fire stops in my throat, for a complete connection between the centers of physical and spiritual creation. The throat chakra starts to move, it's a magnificent kind of whirlwind. I can hear it swirling and vibrating like a tornado.

Then the Serpent starts again from the sacrum; it reaches my head, stops at the pituitary and activates the center.

Suddenly I have my doubts: "Am I ready for a total opening tonight? Oh god, I mustn't stop this process with my questions..."

The throat and the head centers are now working together, my forehead is lightened by a bluish flame, vivid and strong. And I find myself with a quarter of the moon on my 6th chakra, silver-blue, pointing upward. The vibrations of my whole body have changed, the Light is going through the top of my head; the moon shines and two golden globes are placed in my palms. Serene, perfectly happy, I am Myself. Thank you."

***

Thousands of books have been published about the chakras and Hindu thought in terms of Kundalini. Our goal is to introduce the public to the Alta Major Center, which is generally unknown.

The awakening of the Alta Major and its integration within the system of energies creates the merging of the material and spiritual forces, balanced by the heart.

In the present incarnation, I read my first book about Kabbalah at age 24. It was The Mystical Kabbalah of Dion Fortune. From this whole book, I can remember only one line: "In Daath is contained the mystery of regeneration, the key to manifestation."

These words literally struck me; without understanding them completely and intellectually, I was jumping around and laughing, saying: "This is the key, I know, everything is here!" Years later, I happened to read Michel Coquet's book, *Chakras and Initiations*, that contained a few paragraphs on this subject.

Finally, some month ago, as a confirmation of this book, a great deal of which I had already written by then, a friend gave me, as a gift, the book *Kabbalah*, by Charles Poncé, in English. For a long time, I ignored several lines printed on the back cover, sentences that, once more, made be jump for joy when I discovered them.

This is what they said:

"Somewhere, in each of us, there is an Adam, in need of restoration, in exile from the Garden. The goal of Kabbalism is the restoration of divine man through the medium of mortal man. We are, so to speak, both the laboratory and the chemist who works there. All of this is to say that there is an intimate relationship between man and his spiritual counterpart; the mystery of this relationship is to be found in the Sephiroth. If one can learn how to connect the thread that hangs down from the Sephiroth with the thread of one's own being, if one can discover the **opening at the base of the skull**, one may begin the work of the restoration."

Our recommendation to beginners is to read a basic book about chakras in order to study the subject thoroughly. Nevertheless, in order for the reader to follow us, let us stop for a brief summary about the main centers, which is extracted from our book, *Satanic Spiritual Abuse and Spirituality*: "The chakras - wheels - are centers of energy rooted along the spine, with an exteriorization in the front of the body. We will use the internal face of our body to locate them. We will use their names in Sanskrit, along with a translation into English.

The seven chakras that we will discuss are the seven main ones, the best known. We also have minor centers and more subtle chakras connected to our spiritual dimensions. These latter, which are located out of the physical body, will not be dealt in this book.

1. MULADHARA CHAKRA - The coccygeal center. = Root.
   • Element: Earth. Color red. The vowel is a deep, low sound. Mmmmm, using the sound Uh.
   • Located at the base of the spine, between the rectum and the genitalia.
   • Symbol: a 4-petaled lotus - 4 realms
   • Connected to the suprarenal glands (i.e., above the kidneys).
   • This is instinct, the incarnated life principle, the place where the fire of Kundalini lies dormant.
   • Colon. Bone structure.
   • Power. Dependence. Fear.

2. SVADISTHANA. The genital center. = Sweetness
   • Element: water. Color orange. Vowel U.
   • Midway between the pubic area and the navel.
   • A 6-petaled lotus.

- Connected to the gonads and the spleen.
- Sexuality, expression of our basic animal nature, our basic instinctual drives. Creation on a physical level.
- Kidneys, bladder, uterus, reproductive system.
- Trust and self-love.

3. MANIPURA - The solar center. = City of jewels.
    - Element: fire. Color: yellow orange. Vowel: O.
    - 10 petals
    - Situated at the level of the solar plexus.
    - Connected to the pancreas.
    - Center of desires, of "human-instinctive" emotions. Will. Group consciousness.
    - Stomach, digestion, liver, muscles.
    - Desire for control. Self sabotage or motivation. Anger. Feeling of guilt.

4. ANAHATA. Cardiac. "Unstruck," like the sound of a gong that has not been struck.
    - Element: air. Color: green. Vowel: pure aaaah sound. Open sound.
    - 12-petaled lotus.
    - On the level of the heart.
    - Connected to the thymus gland.
    - Cardio-vascular and respiratory systems.
    - Intersection of the so-called inferior and superior centers. Power without love is vain.
    - Love and compassion.

5. VISHUDDHA - Throat. = To purify.
    - Element: ether. Color: blue. Vowel French é as in "café.
    - 16 petals.
    - Larynx area.
    - Connected to the thyroid.

- Communication, creativity, spiritual creation.
- Throat, voice, thyroid problems.
- The energy of this chakra is later transferred to the Alta Major center.

6. AJNA - Frontal. = Knowing or Knowledge.
- Element: the mind. Color: indigo. Vowel: long e as in feel.
- 2-petaled lotus.
- Between the eyes, at the root of the nose.
- Connected to the pituitary gland or hypophysis.
- Mental and psychic abilities. Development of the real self. Intuition. Perception. Clairvoyance.
- Eyes/vision. Headaches. Brain or intellectual abilities.
- Ida and Pinguala meet in the vicinity of the Ajna.

7. SAHASRARA - Coronal, crown chakra = One thousand petals.
- Light element - Color: purple or white. Vowel: the highest-pitched eeeee of a scream.
- 1000 petals.
- Above the crown of the head.
- Connected to the pineal body or epiphysis.
- Seat of Shiva, Consciousness.
- Connected to Mulhadara, the 4 petals multiply them selves and fuse in the divine consciousness.

CHAKRAS AND INFORMATION

The chakras are connected to genetics. By "genetics" we do not mean just the determining factors for an individual's sex or eye color. Recorded in the structure of your chakras is the information acquired, understood, and integrated within your personal frequency. In this particular case, the term genetics is used in an expanded sense, to include your spiritual lineage, your karma, as well as the soul group you are a part of and its collective karma.

Your systems of chakras evolved with the races, according to the vibratory changes of humankind, of the planet and the planetary logos. As an individual, however, you have the opportunity to sail at your own speed and create for yourself a unique nature, to evolve and return to the Whole.

The chakras are immersed in the roots of the inter-planetary existence. They give us access to the universal genetic memories. They are magnetic antennae, connecting you to the external world - individuals, planet, cosmos.

Opening a chakra is to give oneself access to a full range of new information. This information will be processed, screened by the organs in an interaction with the glandular system, which will then produce a renewed quality of energy. This data will then be sent to the blood and cellular level.

The maturing of a chakra creates new frequencies, ones that are capable of digging down into the universal reservoir and that will, in turn, influence the vibrations of the body and the corresponding organs.

In order to assist the evolution of the chakras, a conscious effort of personal purification is required, which enables a progressive maturation from a very materialistic energy to a refined one, which is the spiritualization of matter and form. This work will lead to the creation of threads of light that will mix with the etherical vehicle and slowly penetrate the dense body - from the exterior to the interior. This will result in the creation of the body of Light and then the non-necessity of using a physical instrument.

Light, the basis of creation, includes the data, the information necessary to evolve. These coded elements are spread in the photons and participate in the elaboration of comprehension or data

100

identification zones.

The chakras are also a mass of energy in movement. When they reach a certain power, they are similar to swastikas of light, whose power emanates from the center and propels itself outward.

The centers change both color and form as the individual progresses, parallel to the evolution of the planet. When they are completely formed, the chakras take the configurations and colors that are revealed in the traditional manuscripts and paintings. They manifest themselves as holographic images with beautiful hues, stuck onto the physical body.

The petals of the chakras are the emanations of the thoughts that have been accumulated throughout the ages, at a communal as well as personal level. The centers are connected to the deepest, most secret aspects of the psyche. They are based, indeed built upon the old genetic data like a chalice, whose stem, like a funnel, dives into the roots of existence and presents, indeed externalizes what a person really is.

The chakras are linked to the Kundalini by a maze of nerves, which have an etheric essence. These meridians send their power out into the entire body and prepare for the awakening of the Kundalini-Serpent.

It is not possible to study these energies right now, because they exist in data and knowledge that is still not accessible to human beings because of their coarseness, their lack of vibratory refinement - and their karma, but soon there will be devices to measure these frequencies and allow you to heal them in a different way. This will be similar to genetic manipulations and will probably be performed by the souls who operated centuries ago. Similarly, although you cannot understand how chakras transmit information, the Knowledge will come progressively, if you trust your intuition and sensitivity.

THE CARDIAC CHAKRA

The cardiac chakra is the center that gives access to the Soul. Its opening gives rise to the ray of Love/Creation. It is connected with the third initiation, which brings about the alignment of the terrestrial forces and the forces of the Soul.

The heart is rooted in the three lower chakras, like a flower stem looking up to the sky, propelling its energy upward. Therefore, it is necessary to understand the energies of the first chakras in order to nourish the fourth center.

This is the task that the human race must accomplish both individually and as a group, in order, in the next few years, to move on to the cardiac frequency. The human race has lived with its instinct and has integrated life and sexuality in the way that occurs in the animal kingdom. Humans experience the benefits and the drawbacks inherent in the separation, the duality that leads us to terrestrial procreation and the creativity necessary for the evolution of societies. This is the work of the first two chakras. In order, then, to integrate the energies of the third center, the solar center, we have to find our own identity, the primary awareness of our own self. From this awareness there grows the desire to master the other in order to increase or establish personal power. Thus man has learned the laws of control, the situations of the tyrant or the victim. To master the fourth center, man must bring his drives into equilibrium, must center himself on the awareness and the divine within him.

The germ of the Soul is found in the heart, but in a veiled way; you cannot communicate with it, because you are at the mercy of miasms that give rise to negative terrestrial emotions. The cardiac chakra cannot be fully opened until the subconscious mind has been cleansed of emotional toxins that are the residue of other incarnations/dimensions. It is necessary to clear away anything that stands in the way of pure emotions - emotions that are not based on subconscious ties or on needs. Man must be able to live in himself and through himself, without the expectation that other of the exterior will provide the energies or actions to make him complete.

When romantic love has been experienced and transcended, the "meeting" will be established on the basis of two notes that vibrate in unison, on the subtle link, on the harmony between two chakras or systems that create a third frequency - a creative frequency - the law of triangles. This can happen with the atonement of two individuals, equally free and pure, on a human and spiritual dimension, and it automatically results in a creation on the spiritual plane.

By "pure emotion" we mean the kinds of feelings that have already overcome most human emotions based on the duality in matter. Man, using his physical vehicle, has known a passion that is purely sexual, similar to animal instinct, which has evolved to the ability to love his family and fellow creatures; he is then transmuting his feelings into a love for the other in his divineness and as a group soul.

With the blossoming open of the cardiac chakra, humankind will soon comprehend total communication, the expression of Love/Wisdom, a harmonious and conscious interaction of the different parts of the spiritual body of the soul group.

PRACTICAL EXERCISE

It is recommended that you concentrate on your cardiac chakra during your daily meditation. To "concentrate" does not mean to become fixated on one specific thought. Rather, in starting your meditation, focus on your heart, visualizing a blooming flower and a pink ray entering this area. You might also ask for the presence of Christ in your heart. Then stop thinking altogether; forget everything, simply let your thoughts drift by you like clouds; in silence, rejoin the Source.

CARDIAC AND ROOT CHAKRAS

The cardiac chakra is connected to the root center. In the first chakra there dwells the instinct of life, of incarnation; in the cardiac there lies the germ of life, the immortal soul. Through the path of service and sacrifice, the disciple must spiritualize his energies; then these two centers will work in synergy.

In fact, the soul made a commitment to blossom through the journey into matter, but it cannot be nurtured if the subject does not demonstrate his desire to be alive, to be integrated into the human and terrestrial experience that provokes reactions and emotions. Conversely, the first chakra will be unable to truly extend its roots, to send its energy to the other centers and be a strong base for the construction of the human spiritualized structure, if the heart does not take part, if the emotional structure refuses to cooperate or if there is a state of depression in the individual.

Such a situation can occur - most often is the case with old souls - when these beings are "fed up" with incarnating and are experiencing deep emotional traumas, at a moment when the individual still has not achieved a state of detachment or pure Love.
The soul, living in the very specific conditions of matter, has voluntarily chosen to meet the vibrations of the mineral, animal and human realms. The soul cannot abandon this process, but a temporary state of discomfort, of malaise, will render the

individual incapable of creating in his material life, incapable of responding to his terrestrial needs and living in and with the feelings of security and stability.

Indeed, it is impossible to ignore the feeling, the emotion of life, the communication with others, which is a form of sacrament, a recognition of the self in the other and of God in the other. This emotion, emanating from the cardiac chakra, is the germ that allows for material creation, relating to the first center. Let us keep in mind that in sexual communication and procreation - even if there is no true love between two individuals/energies - there is nonetheless an attraction, a form of emotion. The law of the attraction of the negative and positive polarities is a form of emotion, is a prelude to spiritual and divine Love.

Emotion teaches us. It brings us closer to a spiritual state that allows us to achieve procreation. Spiritual marriage is the fusion of the energies of Matter and Spirit. The union of the emotion (cardiac center) with the vital force (root) begins the exteriorization of creative energy, it gives the impetus, the support that allows the soul to reach the frequency of co-creation/materialization.

In the same way, in order to become creators, human beings must marry the energies of the first and the fourth chakra. When this marriage is made possible by a purification of the other centers and energy channels, then the rising of Kundalini and enlightenment are possible.

Families with a cardiac pathology are generally carrying an unresolved emotional karma. The individual members meet to harmonize their relationships/vibrations and move on to an interaction based on peace.

Gold, one of God's two creative vibrations, helps re-establish the flowing of the vital fluids in the muscle and the cardiac chakra. By "fluids" we do not mean simply the physical ones, but rather the communication of etheric and spiritual energies.

* * *

KUNDALINI

Kundalini means 'Coiled Serpent'. Closely connected with the first chakra, in the nest formed by the sacral vertebrae lays the sleeping Serpent.

Dormant in most of the population, the Serpent looks for its way in the body. Kundalini will follow the path of the main meridians:
- Shushama, in the center, along the spine.
- Ida, on the left, feminine, negative in polarity.
- Pinguala, on the right side, masculine and positive.

All the meditation techniques and especially yoga, prayer, the shamans' and soufis' trances all tend to the manifestation of the primordial Energy in the body and to the Kundalini's awakening. When Kundalini gets through Shushama, she is supposed to destroy all the obstacles to her passage, along the spinal cord. Truly, the Serpent cannot manifest itself if the disciple is not ready to receive him. The initiable has to be purified in his body and spirit, in order for the mechanism to be able to function, and for the powerful Energy coming along with Kundalini to find its way. Projecting herself out of her millenary home, the Serpent floods the body with energy and sets all the chakras on fire. She changes the individual's structure, not only on a physical level, but mainly emotionally, by the revelation of a presence, a frequency, dormant and ignored, far from the Adept's consciousness until then.

Disciples who are traveling along the path are eager for sensations and techniques. There are thousands of books directing you toward different paths, such as yoga or breathing techniques, by which you may raise up the Kundalini. Indian saints have dedicated their lives to the quest for this phenomenon, to the fabulous meeting with the Mother Kundalini. In doing so, they initiate their students in rituals that give rise to a surge of energy in the body, to the point where physical sensations have been induced in people or they have ended up with new psychic powers.

There is still some confusion with regard to Kundalini, both in the minds of the students and in the minds of some teachers.

Kundalini, the coiled Serpent, is a blueprint, a signature. Of course it is part of your genetic code, but because of its nature, it is the hallmark of what your world has been experiencing for thousands of years, and continues to experience even now.

Although your body gives you a physical appearance and sensations, it is still a condensation of forces, of fire, still just an illusion. Above all, we are all made of energy. This shell, this material tool that you are using to experience the illusion of matter, of Separation, is just a small part of a whole. Your astral and spiritual bodies play a predominant role not merely on a human level; remember that under the guidance of your soul, you are multidimensional. This means that other parts of you are evolving in other space/times, with a distinct body and a different awareness. And finally, you are the cells of the grandiose body of an entity, who also lives on several planes, has chakras and a Kundalini at his image.

The most important thing in you, then, is your energetic, complete structure, the configuration and progressive integration of your spiritual nervous system, the development of your chakras or antennae, in the context of the body of a planetary Logos and of the Solar System.

When you are meditating, breathing, subjecting yourself to strenuous mental or physical exercise, you are progressively changing your thoughts; you are taking control instead of floating gently along in your astral/emotional body. By means of your brain, you are building a whole different world of thoughts, new energies that are more subtle, stronger.

What you feel or see during these sessions is the energy that you have created or modified to the point that it became palpable, tangible. This force, of a unique nature but with multiple manifestations, uses the pathways existing within your body, that is to say the meridians, nadis. It will inundate your glands, illuminate the caverns of the brain. This energy will give you a feeling of strength, out-of-body experiences, orgasmic outbreaks. It will drive you on to different states of consciousness.

But this energy, even if it is part of Kundalini, is not Kundalini.

It is obvious, when you do meet the Serpent, that you cannot confuse it with any ascending movement of energy, of an orgasmic or luminous type.

Kundalini is the revelation of a signature, of your belonging to a world that, with a derision that is typically human, you decided to drive out of your minds and hearts.

Just stop for a moment and take a look at all the statues in India, in China, the representations of the saints and the gods. What do you see if not the Serpent, the One who was given the right to govern the earth, to give mankind his own imprimatur.

Welcoming Kundalini is to give her, finally, the opportunity to wake up. It means to give to the Adepti, the Revelation, in their own bodies, undisputed, extreme, of the Great Secret. Kundalini, at the root of the energetic mechanism of the human chakras, is a serpent. It is the powerful emanation of the energy that rules the planet earth, the reptoid energy, the mark, the signature of the Serpent.

BAPTISM OF MATTER

Matter in which the Nameless One projected his Spirit, was also containing the darkness, from which the reptoid civilization, the Serpent is an emanation.

"God saw that the light was good; and God separated light from darkness." Genesis 1:4.

The purification of the channels of energy does not occur without an understanding of the pairs of opposites or complements: beauty and ugliness, peace and war, hot and cold, GOOD and EVIL, LIGHT and DARKNESS. You were experiencing the war within you, the confrontation of the non-integrated energies of Light and Darkness. Then you understood and balanced the energy in the two central meridians, Ida and Pinguala. This force, whose total frequency is made up of the harmony of opposites, will merge, rise up in one flow, in one unique channel, in the center of the spinal column.

Seeing and experiencing the manifestation of the Serpent means recognizing your own origin. It is to accept the fact that human matter was submitted to the double frequency, Ying/Yang, White/Black, vibration equally manifested in DNA with double helixes.

To confess to this inheritance, the necessity of the two antagonistic energies that form the whole, allows for the opening of the spiritual eye and the discovery of the secret of the serpent, whom religions have always raised up to the status of the evil one, the adversary. He is the adversary because he manifests the other side, the other vibration, the other side of the creator God, who is revealed in the Cosmos.

"God said to Adam: But of the tree of the knowledge of good and evil, thou shalt not eat of it: for in the day that thou eatest thereof thou shalt surely die."

The awareness that occurs through the fall into matter means death. To live in the state of incarnation, of matter, is of course to be going through cycles of creation/destruction. Death is inherent in matter, but contains life in itself.

THE ROLE OF THE SERPENT

This is what the serpent means when he whispers into Eve's ear: "Ye shall not surely die: For God doth know that in the day ye eat thereof, then your eyes shall be opened, and ye shall be as gods, knowing good and evil." The serpent recalls his role as Bringer of Light. He is the one who gave man the opportunity of awareness, for the reintegration in Conscious Light.

In the Tradition, the Serpent appears at the dawn of creation. "The spirit of God moving above the Chaos" is described as a serpent sparking fire and light. The Absolute manifests in cycles. The first cycle in the creation is the one of the non-manifested; the second cycle, the manifestation, then of the projection of Spirit into matter, which is densification. During this period, the Reptoid civilization appeared. The reptiles, the dragons, are still present on earth. They manifest in an intrinsically way or in the form that some species take during their growing process.

In all the mythologies, the Serpent is the holder of Wisdom, the

Initiator. The planetary logos is surrounded of 4 Lipikas or Lords of Karma. "The closest of our Planetary Logos, is named the Live Serpent and his emblem is a blue serpent, with, on his head, an eye in the shape of a rubis." Alice Bailey.

Spirit was given to the animal-man with the advent of the Sanat Kumara and the Hierarchy which accompanies him as karmic group. This allowed the human race to accomplish a leap in evolution and to prepare itself for self-consciousness. The mind is characterized by the faculty of discrimination, or capability to make choices between Good and Evil. Man has to evolve between the pairs of opposites, and to find his balance by experiencing and making conscious decisions. The framework for this work is matter, out of the edenic garden.

What does this mean in terms of your spiritual search? Kundalini is not the goal in itself. Rather, it is a Revelation, a phase, a momentum in the Self, in moving toward the meeting of the real Self.

You have been preparing yourself over a number of incarnations; you have solved your most serious emotional and astral problems; you have cleansed your body/mind of most of the miasmas related to the journey on earth.

Your energy system is ready, your body is capable of receiving the influx of the Kundalini. Capable of the Silence of the Knower, your are emotionally able to read and assimilate the lesson on the mode of Will and Unconditional Love. Kundalini is knocking at your door. Triumphant matter is baptizing your most intimate self, is finding its way inside you and is about to salute the Spirit. It is the Spiritual Marriage.

It is the discovery of the presence of the Serpent within you, that

111

you have to assimilate as your heredity, in the systemic genes of the spiritual group you belong to, as a citizen of Earth, inhabitant of matter.   It is the redemption that we are all expected to live through and concede to, in accepting the burden of incarnation, by the presence of the this image which was deformed and twisted, to the point to becoming sin and abomination.

SECTION THREE : PERSONAL TRANSMUTATION

1. THE SHADOW

I met Bill at a party. He was about 30 years old, with little spiritual education, innocuous. Very soon we were talking about the effect of the Shadow on the planet. Seen through clairvoyance, it was obvious that this man, although very nice and peaceful as a person, had a very powerful double, one that was extremely black, sexual and overbearing. I let him express himself and suddenly he blurted out:

"I think I know what you mean. I have a friend, very sensitive and psychic; although we're very good friends, we've never had an actual sexual relationship. One night, however, this young woman, saw me in her room in an astral projection. What bothers and frightens me somewhat is that then I had sex with her, but in an extremely violent and unexpectedly dominating way. Mina couldn't stop me or reduce the aggression or the pain I was inflicting upon her. She was injured and ended up needing treatment. The gynecologist who examined her, obviously thinking that this had been a real physical contact, warned her about such violent sex."

Bill added: " I deeply believe in the reality of this aspect of myself. What can I do to stop being this person?"

When night came, I knew that I would rejoin Bill and help him, on the other side. I programmed myself before sleep and set a lighted candle beside me. In the morning, he called me up:

"I have to tell you what happened last night. Although I couldn't see you, I knew that you were with me, to help me cleanse my

113

spiritual self. I met my shadow and told him that I refused to participate in such acts, becoming aggressive like that and raping woman at night. I asked my shadow to leave me."

***

The Judeo-Christian exoteric tradition is based on the principles of good and evil, of heaven and hell; God has a famous adversary, Satan. In the Oriental philosophy, we are taught about the existence of two opposite and complementary forces, Yin and Yang.

In India and in Africa, the notion of good and evil is not stated in the same way that it is in the classical doctrine of the Bible. For instance, the god Shiva is called the 'Howler'. A deity who is both benevolent and malevolent, he is simultaneously the healer and the Destroyer.

In numerous traditional ceremonies, the healer, the sorcerer, is the one who saves lives and also the one capable of taking them away. The question of power and the use of the laws of nature — which some call magic — goes far beyond the strict limits of the Judeo-Christian education and patriarchal group consciousness.

The system of beliefs that we have had for thousands of years has shaped a pattern for a specific type of behavior, a more or less subtle form of consciousness, based on the principles of good and evil. In fact, even left to his own devices, without any education, a human being, deeply seeded in his heart, has the germ of Consciousness. Man distinguishes himself from the animal kingdom through his faculties of reason, his ability to learn and then use sound judgment.

CONSCIOUSNESS

The goal of the creature is not only to refine his consciousness, but also to reach Consciouness by the "Co-knowledge," the revelation of his true nature. (In French, knowledge is Connaissance, a word that we can divide into Co-Naissance - Naissance is Birth. Then, Co-Naissance litterally means Co-Birth, a new Birth induced through awareness).

God discovered himself in the process of mirror-Creation. The creation reaches Consciousness through individualization; it has to differentiate itself from the reservoir of the Spirit.

At the moment when one separates himself from God/the spirit, one enters this zone of the created, of matter. In our system, the Rays, which emanate from the Absolute, are the positive aspects of manifestation that are projecting themselves in the negative matter. From the very beginning, a pattern was projected, based on the necessity of two antagonists energies in order for there to be creation.

The disciple's quest is the search for a higher level of consciousness, the recognition of these two forces or polarities in himself and on the outside. Is there any limit to the exploration of the laws of attraction/repulsion that rule the world, through Consciousness? What about heaven? What can heaven be for us with regard to the extension of awareness, of consciousness?

"Then your eyes shall be opened, and ye shall be as gods, knowing good and evil."

Paradoxically, these are the words of Satan, the one who is supposed to represent the Shadow.

It is necessary to pass through the Shadow in order to become Conscious Light.

WHAT, IN FACT, IS THE SHADOW?

The Absolute, in its Essence, is Spirit. The creation is the manifestation of the Spirit. It creates matter that is a complement to or opposite of the spirit. Matter is a concretization, a condensation. The phenomenon of densification of the light suppresses a number of the photons and reduces the possibility of receiving information on the created object. The lowering of the level of information, of consciousness, induces a lower frequency and the extension of the zones of the shadow. The shadow is a lack of information, a non-consciousness, the distortion or disappearance of the Light of the Spirit. This situation might be described as being momentary, because the raison d'être of the shadow is:

- To create time,
- To reveal the light,
- To be enlightened,
- To return to the original light.

By projecting Himself, the Absolute creates a mirror, the other aspect of himself. It is the beginning of the Duality. The creation manifests itself in duality, in the extension/retraction, or the movement that turned to itself.

The Creation expresses Duality by the opposites or complementaries. All the colors have a theoretical complementary; all notes, feelings and emotions are balanced by their opposites.

God, the Absolute, is manifested in the whole range of his created work. In fact, he allows the existence of all the vibrations, all the frequencies, which are materializations of his Word, the Sound or Logos. These frequencies hold the entire spectrum of the terrestrial notes, from the lightest to the densest, from the purest to the darkest.

HOW DOES THE BEING INCORPORATE THE SHADOW?

There are many ways to consider this problem; we would like to open up new possibilities within you.

Let us go back to the very first moments of Creation. Let us try to imagine the beginning. In the void, there is Source. Source starts his extension in the Infinite. It is the first movement, the first current.

Source starts duplicating Himself, starts creating. We emerge from Source, individualizing, in the form of a spark, Life, a distinct Soul, separated from the Origin. As soon as we are out of Source, we are no longer pure Spirit. We go away, step by step, initiating an opposite force; we integrate atoms, matter. And the more we ingest matter, density, the more we load ourselves with shadow.

Thus we go farther and farther, and multiply our experiments. At the very beginning, we are an energy, much more subtle than the human body. But each time that we hit opposite, conflicting forces, we modify the vibration, the texture of our Self. We integrate the movement and the flow, and then the resistance. We assimilate the polarities. Life, away from Source, expresses itself within the duality, or expression of the opposites.

The experiment will continue for millions of years. The more time passes, the more shadow we carry. In a concrete way, this means that you become involved in brutal, difficult, violent incarnations. Like a musician who plays thousands of imperfect scales before being able to interpret a harmonious symphony, all the difficulties, all the mistakes are allowed and indeed are a part of the game. We will choose to live in the shadow in order to understand and integrate its vibrations. We were probably weak, liars, tyrants, murderers; we practiced sorcery and black magic to satisfy our need for personal power. All of this is keeping us so far from Spirit that we lose sight of ourselves. We forget the primordial Spark, who we really are; we do not even remember Source. Then we get ourselves into inextricable situations, we do foolish things, suffer when the Spark is shining deep within us. Sometimes, we feel lost, we rebel.

The pendulum always makes a complete movement before it returns to its starting point. You went to the final extreme in experiencing physicality; now it is time to re-ascend and to nourish yourselves with lightness and with light, in order for you to return to the Spirit. But this time, when you rejoin Source, you will be Conscious.

Nowadays, you are probably a refined, balanced and non-violent person. Apparently, you no longer need to express basic brutality, hatred or racism, or wage war. You are willing to find enlightenment, and already you manifest yourself through your heart.

Nevertheless, as long as you are incarnated, in your physical vehicle you will still bear the imprint of your past/parallel experiences. You vibrate on a peculiar note, which is the sum of all these adventures on Earth and in all the areas of the Universe where you have been living. This frequency that you broadcast from deep down within yourself is composed of the entire spectrum of the colors/vibrations that you have ever known and that are recorded in your genetic computer, DNA.

Before returning to the Light, to the Spirit, in the Conscious Co-

Awareness, you must come into contact with your deep and total self, in order to see, touch, understand and transmute any residues from the Shadow. Only the "meeting" makes the marriage possible. The discovery of the Shadow heralds the merging with the Light.

ARE THE SHADOW AND THE KARMA NEGATIVE?

Yes, with regard to their polarities.
No, with regard to their essence.

You are human beings. You express yourselves in a world and with a language that are both adapted and transformed by the system you live in and the education you have had. Now, the word "negative" is psychologically charged, in a subjective way. Women have gone so far as to refuse the idea of holding a so-called negative polarity. You have to return to simple and basic notions. After all, you accept the fact that electrons have a positive or negative charge, with the consequences that this has on the nature of electricity or the atom. Well, now it's time to recognize the duality within you.

The words "shadow" and "karma" merely convey facts, as a result of the nature of the Being. Here we are, in fact, dealing with the nature of being, that creature that it is. And here I use a capital letter, for I am also speaking of the nature of God.

Through the act of creation, in replicating himself and projecting the spark of Life outside Himself, God has generated the Shadow and the Karma. He did not create the excess of the Shadow; rather, he has allowed for the existence of matter and the appearance of polarities. The lack of awareness, of comprehension, of consciousness are the conditions leading to what we might call a cluster or an accumulation of shadow. The dark side of the universe was created by the conscious decision to hide information,

119

to hide the possibility of an increased awareness.

The solution is and will be a harmony, a balance between the polarities. Based on the exchange, on a free flow of positive and negative energies, harmony cannot produce any of those things that we are accustomed to calling evil.

SHADOW AND SPIRIT

In this chapter we want to come back to a notion that was touched on earlier. Millions of years ago, in Lemuria, the human race reached a state of evolution that we might describe as intermediary.

The human body was partially densified. Because of the third eye, which was still intact, man could communicate freely with dimensions that are now forbidden to him. The spirits, the devas, were his companions. Man was in close contact with his essence/soul; but he had to condense even more, to go further down into the zones of densification of primordial matter. This meant having a physical body in which the divine would be present only as a germ or a memory. This is what we call the Fall.

The Fall does not concern only the human race. In the past, those spiritual entities who agreed to participate in the creation and to take a physical body found themselves in a similar situation, agreeing to follow the law of karma.

At the same time as the acquisition of a body and the severing of the natural and easy connection to the divine, another important process took place. The creature had already assimilated the vibrations of the three realms, animal, vegetable and mineral. Now he had to evolve into a completely human stage, which implied the faculty of thought. Without thought, without the mind, the

Being cannot experience the phenomenon of Consciousness. The mind, the ability to discriminate, was then vitalized by the transfer of the energy of the Sanat Kumara onto the planet.

According to Alice Bailey, "discrimination is the educatory process to which the Self itself is in the process of developing intuition — that faculty whereby the Self recognizes its own essence in and under all forms. Discrimination concerns the duality of nature, the Self and the not-Self and is the mean of their differentiation in the process of abstraction. The intuition concerns unity and is the capacity of the Self to contact other selves, and is not a faculty whereby the not-self is contacted." *Treatise On Cosmic Fire.*

Two realities are created by this process:
- The recognition of the duality and of existence in this context. The faculties of the Mind allow us to discern that matter is just a creation, an illusion, a mirror.
- The acquisition of intuition, which lets us find our way back to the All in One.

Without using discrimination, the being cannot be conscious of his individuality, or the difference between himself/herself and the other, the external world. The second step will be to recognize that the Self is multiple, infinite, One.

I AM THAT I AM

WOMAN AND SHADOW

Woman, negative polarity, right brain, intuition, the subconscious mind, the moon, the dark moon...

In antiquity, before the kingdom of Yaweh, woman was the receptor of and the contact with the divine. Being closer to the other side, because of her structure, the receptacle of life, she communicated knowledge and the secrets of life. Priestess, goddess, natural friend of the Serpent, she initiated man through the sacred marriage and created completeness.

In unison with the slow disintegration of the ties to the divine, the human race convinced itself of the primary role of the mind, of Cartesian logic, using the left brain, the masculine. History, in maintaining and consolidating the power of these religious beliefs, has been transformed, strengthening the kingdom of masculine polarity.

Woman, stripped of honor and having had her rights taken from her, became an object of shame, being saddled with the reputation of being unstable. The flow of life and blood in her body has been tarnished. Even deprived of the right to own a soul, her only role — because this is irreplaceable — has been to become inseminated, without pleasure or divine ecstasy, in order to perpetuate the race.

From priestess and healer, friend of the moon, woman became the sorceress and her gifts became anathema. The moon, divine companion of the sun, pouring out its soft silver glimmer, is now only a symbol of the night, of the malefic shadow. Even more dangerous is the somber, melancholy moon, the goddess with a dark skin who burrows into the forbidden cellars of some churches and gives welcome only to cursed pilgrims.

Woman feels the influence of the moon more deeply before and during her menses. At this moment, she enters a phase of interiorization, into the depths of the subconscious mind, where she meets the dark moon. She experiences a small death, a complete regeneration of her whole structure, obvious not only by means of her period but also in her whole body and emotional state. All the hidden parts of the self are emphasized and brought back to consciousness. At this moment, woman will feel sorrow, frustration and anger; she will have suicidal thoughts, all her emotions stifled deep inside her guts, an expression of her shadow.

This period that women have always regarded to be a burden can actually become a treasure if a woman decides to use it in the way of the wise women of the past.

Woman is invited to pay attention to all the growling and cries that rise up from deep down within her and to search for the cause of her sorrow. The feelings that she is experiencing at this moment are related to hidden memories or parts of herself that she has been repressing — because of her education, the judgment of others or traumatizing situations.

Let us not forget that it is when the moon is dark, when we no longer see her face, that the queen of the night is contemplating the sun, her husband. The alchemic marriage is taking place once again, and it will show us the way.

WHAT IS THE EXPRESSION OF THE SHADOW?

Saul of Tarsis said: "The fruits of the spirit are love, joy, peace, good-will, patience, kindness....sweetness..."

We also read, "Now the works of the flesh are manifest, which are these: Adultery, fornication, uncleanness, lasciviousness, idolatry, witchcraft, hatred, variance, emulations, wrath, strife, seditions, heresies." Galatians: 5, 19-22.

Although these words have Biblical overtones, they reflect the distortion of the intimate being, the darkening of the vibration of the Soul, creating situations of conflict and an animosity toward the self and others.

The Shadow is materialized in each of us by all these parts of our being that move us toward pain, frustration, failure and a lack of Light.

Your responsibility, in order to prepare for the Initiation, is to have the courage to meet your shadow and then to enlighten it, so that the Spirit will transmute the flesh in an expression of Love. The meeting, driven by the feelings of love and acceptance, is the start of a relationship and then of a marriage.

You must create this supreme alchemy in you, whose reward is pure Gold. When two antagonistic energies are completely known, weighed, integrated and balanced, they create the Divine Fire, the Conscious Light.

How can you discover your Shadow? Through a journey into the abyss of the subconscious mind, in perfect integrity.

The process remains the same, remarkably simple and yet extremely complex. You will have to become a detective of sorts, as honestly as possible. Above all, have no shame or fear, for in doing so, you would only increase the Shadow.

2. THE SUBCONSCIOUS MIND

While you are reading this chapter, have a pen and piece of paper on hand in order to write down any observations that come to mind.

"The human being works on three different levels:

- The conscious mind, related to the mental plane.
- The subconscious mind, the inferior mental plane, connected to the emotions.
- The unconscious, where all the knowledge is stored that is innate to you and that you have no mastery of; knowledge that has not yet surfaced in your conscious mind."

The subconscious mind is a part of your internal mechanisms; it relies on instincts and emotions, as well as genetic or acquired programs. The subconscious controls the human mind — your thoughts — and it influences all your actions and aspects of your life. It is an emanation of the astral/emotional body; conversely, it contributes to the development of this astral/emotional body.

The subconscious mind helps create the image you project outwardly, this side of yourself that other people pick up on, which in turn will determine your relationships with others and other aspects of your daily life.

On a strictly spiritual level, a being cannot really evolve unless he has understood — and then healed — the drives of his subconscious mind. To do this means purifying one's astral body and no longer living in an emotional way, but rather according to the mental and spiritual planes.

The subconscious mind is open and ready to record information that is triggered by any emotional stimulation. The keys to this "miracle-computer" are any powerful feelings - fear, happiness, pain, anger, hatred, intense excitement, etc. The doors to the subconscious mind will open wide as soon as you find yourself feeling hurt, betrayed, physically or emotionally battered, or powerless in the face of an adversary or a situation; this mechanism is also triggered by the influence of stimulants such as alcohol, drugs, and sex.

The subconscious mind is a mechanism without a real mind; it is blind and stubborn, lacking in any wisdom. Its only way of functioning is to record images, sensations and feelings and to connect them to each other, without trying to interpret or classify them in any logical or reasonable way.

Examples: "While you are eating a chocolate cake, your kitten is run over. In the future, any chocolate cake will give you nausea.

The man who raped you wore a red tie or had very wide-set eyes. Now all red ties or wide-set eyes will either frighten or attract you by means of the subconscious lessons you have learned, which generate your actual patterns."

All religious and political groups manipulate the subconscious mind of their new members in order to sway them, imprint their minds and then appropriate their actions and energy.

Hitler, under the influence of negative entities, was a master in this regard. First, the crowd was subjected to an intense psychological underpinning - propaganda, power, fear. Then, every means possible was used to access the mind of his audience:
     - The number of participants in a given event has a tendency to create an emotionally charged energy. People feel part of a group, a fraternity, protected or ready to act.
     - The creation of a given setting, the use of a ritual, the use

of symbols, flags, music.

- The personality, the tone of the voice, generally powerful, magnetic, hypnotic.

- Underlying sensations of tyranny and fear.

- A call to occult forces.

Religious organizations use the same methods, adding the belief that God is supposedly speaking through the medium of a priest or a preacher.

The initiations given by mystical groups or by certain gurus are aimed at reaching the subconscious mind and gaining access to the minds of their disciples. The ambiance created by the need for devotion and the feeling of belonging to a group, emblems and symbols that are generally unknown to the apprentice, a specific vocabulary, the use of incense, music, sounds — everything is set up so that the subconscious mind will be opened and programming or beliefs will be implanted in it.

In fact, any initiation ceremony tends to have enough of an impact on the participants to reach the secret inner workings of the personality.

The power of the subconscious mind over the individual has contributed greatly to keeping humankind in Maya, the illusion. Most of you, without being aware of it, go through life wearing a mask. The personality that you show outwardly is rarely an extension or copy of your intimate thoughts, fears, habits, which are in fact the basis of your real behavior, the one that externalizes itself and creates your life environment.

In the outer world, you act according to acquired patterns, social necessities educational systems. You learn that you are not supposed to speak in the presence of a given person; you are not supposed to whistle or sing in the street, or get angry. But anything hidden within the subconscious mind will rise to the surface in the event of a shock or an emotion — just as soon as the right button is pushed. And, because you are do not experience your own reality openly, the feeling you project to others is twisted, creating an unstable vibration, or even one that is distorted and violent.

A. THE EFFECT OF THE SUBCONSCIOUS MIND IN YOUR LIFE

1. CONTROL OF YOUR LIFE

The subconscious mind controls your existence and prevents you from being fully connected to your soul. Your life might be a succession of events that are not in harmony with the standards of your spirit or with projects that you are working on. Although you have shown yourself to others as being a quiet and controlled person, you are unable to be stable, happy, successful and in good health. If your problem is even stronger, your life is probably a succession of catastrophes, both physical and emotional, and of painful events you cannot escape — events that do not always reflect your "surface" personality.

All these experiences are a reflection of an internal battle that you must understand — and then stop — in order to make real progress along the path of the initiation.

2. INCONGRUENCE

You are confused, unable to make a decision. Your life is incoherent, you find it is inconsistent with the principles you believe in. Often, you lack judgment and wisdom. You are unable, at least sometimes, to live up to your standards and, in particular, the dictates of your conscience.

Below are some examples of what we mean, albeit slightly exaggerated for effect:

- A very refined woman, a practicing Catholic, who suddenly participates in orgies or begins having sex with every taxi-driver she meets.

- A guru who cannot resist creating a harem, or a system in which he must "initiate" his disciples, regardless of what their sex is.

- Or, even more amusing because it's so typically human: an old Hindu wise man who is unable to resist a certain type of woman.

And finally, a sad example:
- The murderer who kills under the impetus of a memory, of a fear, or a full moon, and who will possibly forget everything he has done.

3. WHO DO YOU ATTRACT?

Your emotional body is the first thing that others perceive when you connect; therefore, a subconscious problem will cause you attract individuals who do not meet your standards or wishes.

Conversely, you are unable to meet:
- The person of your dreams
- The friends or relationships to whom you are willing to ex press yourself.
- The professional contacts that you need.

Example: You are looking for a loving, natural woman, ready to have a family, somewhere in the country. But all you meet - and fall in love with - are *femmes fatales*, overbearing women who like to live in the city, but hate baby bottles and diapers.

4. UNWANTED EMOTIONS

Although you are a disciple on the right path, with pure intentions and a heart focused on the light, you have emotional drives that are both embarrassing and incomprehensible:

- Sudden, uncontrolled anger.
- Fear, phobias, panic attacks or anguish.
- Thoughts of suicide.
- Sadness, depression, anxiety without any apparent cause.
- Shyness, lack of self-confidence or trust.
- Sexual issues - hyper or hypo activity and inclinations.
- Inability to feel.

5. ENTITIES

You attract low-level entities, ones that are not connected to the Light. These beings will remain attached to your body as a burden that interferes with your health and daily life. Possibly, you are often confronted with magicians or sorcerers who work for the dark side of the universe. You happen to be fascinated by or sensitive to any black magic, and have trouble protecting yourself.

B. FINDING THE MECHANISMS OF YOUR SUBCONSCIOUS MIND

1. LIFE PATTERNS

The patterns are an imprint on your subconscious mental mechanisms that induce specific behaviors, habits and situations that come back into your life with some regularity. They are the result of emotions and situations from the past.

Childhood, which actually begins at the time of conception and includes prenatal life, is the most important period with regard to the development of the personality and life patterns. Although already polluted by heredity, a child is a neutral screen that will receive hundreds of visual, tactile, oral, olfactory and emotional impressions. He cannot and indeed does not try to understand them; rather, he records them and creates a world, a system of beliefs, a way to respond and protect himself from his surroundings.

All during his life, or at least until he confronts his subconscious mind, the being will try to re-create the situations that nourished or poisoned him, without making any differentiation. Obstinately, you feel a need to 'be back home.' Just as your grandmother's apple pie always seems to be the best, you will try to reproduce around you the ambiance, the problems and the characters of your childhood.

EXAMPLES:

Lilian had an alcoholic father. Because her mother ended up leaving home, Lilian soon began to feel responsible for her father, whom she helped for many years; she was not, however, able to change his addiction.

As an adult, she only meets and falls in love with alcoholics or drug addicts, whom she desperately wants to rescue. Of course, she fails; in a final burst of courage, she always leaves them . . . only to start over again with a similar story.

At home the ambiance was cold and tense. Nobody was able to speak in a loving manner. You were unable to do anything together without fighting. Now, you have problems in creating a harmonious, loving family. Without any real motive, each time you start to do something with your family, a wave of panic sweeps over you and one of you ends up becoming angry.

Well, you were not born into a given family by chance. Since your first incarnation, you have given yourself energetic and psychological structures. Your evolution as a soul means you have to comprehend the entire range of emotions and vibrations by means of experience. In this regard, your parents give you:

- A framework and vibratory qualities that must confront you in order for you to balance your energies. This means that they will be the instruments to show the problems that you are required to solve. Understanding and overcoming these situations will change not only your reaction toward life but also your mold, the configuration of your energies.

- Genes that correspond to the physical and mental qualities that you are willing to explore within your lifetime. If you wish to experience obesity or tuberculosis, you must, of course, pick parents with the corresponding physical background. If you are to be a martial arts master or a genius in music, you will find a family in which you will, at least, be able to get the required education in this particular field.

- Your parents are generally members of your astral or spiritual family. You meet them because you share unfinished business with them from a past or parallel life, and the cycle must be completed. Your parents are part of your karma. Your responsibility, then, is to free yourself from all your ties to them, whether they be positive or negative.

The most serious patterns are not programmed from your childhood, but rather from your past or parallel lives. The final goal of incarnation is to balance the polarities, manifested on earth as masculine and feminine. In fact, they are two expressions of energy, the dynamic and the receptive ones.

Since your separation from the source, you have had a number of occasions to participate in experiences based on the dynamic or receptive mode. In the beginning, you were just a thinking energy that floated on the cosmic waves — a receptive state. Then you wanted to learn how to resist cosmic movement - dynamic polarity. The successive decisions that you have made with regard to experimenting with forces, the very precise situations that you have experienced have, little by little, sculpted the being that you are today. You have been confronted with circumstances that have hurt or frightened you. You have had a taste of power, sorrow and violence. Through all these events, you have developed tendencies or patterns that you finally reproduce from one incarnation to the other. In doing so, you have been building for yourself an envelope, a denser and denser body. The time is now to make a clean sweep and change, so that your personalities can finally achieve equilibrium.

2. BEING AWARE OF THE PATTERNS
THAT SHAPE YOUR LIFE

We suggest that you start by writing out the answers to the

questions listed below, being as honest as possible. Your answers will serve you as a reference in the future, so you will be able to see the progress you have made. Later, it will be enough for you to make a mental note of a pattern that appears or recurs, in order to help you erase it from the subconscious mind.

Note any unwanted but recurring situations or events that do not correspond to your wishes or inner ethic.

- Marriage or relationships

All the partners you choose seem to have the same problems. What problems are these?

Examples: Liar, cheater, weak, unable to express any tenderness, cold, premeditating, slightly fanatical, unwilling to marry, not in tune with you sexually, permanently unemployed, too handsome and only interested in their looks, overgiving in exchange for blind adoration, always blue-eyed when you prefer brown eyes, do not belong to your social level, live with their mother or their tribe...

They push you into similar situations. What situations are these?

Example: As soon as you start living with someone, they lose their job.

You cannot fall in love without totally giving up your identity.

You are aggressive, anxious, introverted, you burst out in anger any time your partner comes home late.

- Profession

If you are ambitious, do you feel you have reached the level of success you have aspired to? If not, do you think that your life and achievements match your abilities? For example, what if you happen to be very gifted in several areas and yet never try to use your potential. Why?

Whatever your qualifications and degrees, you live in a small seedy apartment and make just enough money to pay your bills. Although you have plenty of ideas, you never finish anything. Why?

Are you a perpetual failure; are you fired every six months? Is it a habit for you to seek out bosses or employees who give you grief or push you into fits of anger - suppressed anger, of course - or who will reenact with you unthinkable situations of abuser/victim.

- Situations, phobias

What are the situations in your daily life that your fear most but that seem to come back with disarming regularity?

Examples: You are afraid of dogs, red-headed women, waves, traffic jams, and yet you have an alarming tendency to keep attracting dogs, red-headed women, tempests, accidents.

You dream of a peaceful, harmonious life, in a cheerful, light yellow house, but instead of this, you have a chaotic existence, surrounded by angry people, and you keep renting only dull and gloomy apartments.

C. PRACTICE

Take out a sheet of paper that you have separated into 2 columns. In the left-hand column, list those situations from your childhood, especially the difficult ones, where you felt hurt, traumatized, when you lost confidence or experienced guilt.

In the right-hand column, write down what decision you made after or because of a given situation or event, a conclusion about yourself or your life in the future. Unfortunately, this is not always a conscious process.

Examples:

- Your father used to beat your mother/ All the men are violent; it is normal to be beaten by a mate.

- You have been unfairly treated by a teacher for a whole year/ there is no justice. I become a rebel, I hide my actions.

- You have been molested or abused by an adult/ I was responsible for this, I am not worth anything/ I am dirty. If the situation kept recurring/ I am a prostitute.

- Your mother left home with another man/all women leave their mate or they are all prostitutes.

When you are finished, compare this list with the patterns that shape your life. Are you discovering obvious similarities?

***

Childhood situations	Decision	Problem in my actual life
My father used to beat my mother	All men beat their mate	I am living with violent men
I was always home alone	I do not deserve to have friends	Loneliness in adult life
You have to be beautiful to find a man	I am only concerned with my look	I live with superficial individuals
My father/mother were always right	I do not know anything/ I am not worth it	Nobody can love me No self confidence
My mother died when I was 6	I deserve to be abandoned I have to live by myself	All my mates leave me. 10 people died around me within 4 years
My father used to beat us every night	Evenings are dangerous	I sleep with a pillow over my head. Every night, I feel like being violent.
You will never do anything with your life	He is right, I am not good at anything	I am never successful. I am a failure.

1. YOU ATTRACT MIRRORS

You have probably noticed that by chance you meet people whose weaknesses upset you. "Birds of a feather flock together." Right, but this tendency is a tool used by your Higher Self/Soul to show you something that you cannot discern naturally, or that you have repressed. For instance, your last friends were:

Angry:
Are you angry or is it difficult for you to admit it? Did you, for reasons unknown even to you, repress your anger? What was the

origin of this feeling?
Violent:
Were violence or abuse present in your normal surroundings?
What are you trying to recreate as an adult?

Liars:
Who was the liar in your house? Who do you look alike? Or, are you lying to yourself?

In fact, in order to heal your personality and change your life, you have to become alert, aware, and make the firm decision to control life instead of being its victim. Conversely, too much control would also be a mistake. As a matter of fact, after having understood a problem, the secret for success is to be able to let go, to move harmoniously in the natural flow of occurrences.

As soon as you are aware of the functioning of the mind and the subconscious, use any moment, any encounter as a lesson, especially if it is a disagreeable one. Any painful or negative emotion reveals a part of the self in need of attention. Always ask yourself this question: "What is the message of my interlocutor? Is my soul trying to tell me something?"

Another way to determine your subconscious problems is to pay attention to your tastes in terms of entertainment, especially movies and books. What are the subjects that touch you, move you? What are your favorite subjects, characters? Why? What do they evoke in you? What memories do you have, agreeable and/ or painful? Are you aware of any problems connected to these topics, that you have not resolved or even dealt with?

Also, think about your sexual tendencies. The body is a temple that your treat with honor, pleasure is natural. But the way you act with your partners conveys your deepest feelings. What leads

138

you to pleasure? What parts of your body seem to be the most sensitive, most linked to sexuality? Do you express your love with your body, or just with words? When you make love, are only physical feelings involved, or do you respond with your heart?

2. SUB-PERSONALITIES

When someone, especially a child, is deeply moved, frightened, traumatized, and cannot bear or handle a situation without doing harm, the brain makes the decision to black out, to repress the event in the maze of your memory. If the trauma is repeated or in similar situations, the child, and then the adult, will react by regularly escaping into a type of amnesia. Little by little, another character emerges, one that experiences the trauma, but this personality is immediately forgotten as soon as the bad time is over. In the future, the survivor will alternate between several lives or personalities, consciously or not, or will switch out according to the emotions he is going through.

When you call into questions your personality patterns again in this chapter, you will know why you eventually created one or several characters. These exercises might also evoke a remembering process. If your own childhood was rather challenging, we suggest you get professional help.

3. ASTRAL SUB-PERSONALITIES

Several cases are possible:

- An ordinary reaction to being treated badly, especially in children, is to leave the body. The victim decides temporarily to leave his physical vehicle and take refuge in the astral or the spiritual dimensions. Splitting becomes a habit. In daily life, one separates to escape uncomfortable or uninteresting situations. The game becomes more complicated, since the subconscious mind made the decision to come up with a personality, a persona, that will split on the astral plane to solve daily problems. Then, the thirst for power, revenge, sexual drives, delicate situations, especially those in complete breach with the self that one has decided to show, will be transposed on the astral plane and lived in secret.

- When the problem does not reach the consciousness, these personalities, which are an integral part of the entire being, will remain alive, beyond physical death and time. They will build their own world, they will create a story that will unfold as a parallel to human life. Contacts will be made with the physical world sporadically, generally through serious or difficult situations. Also this might occur through dreams or artistic expression.

The night is an opportune time for the appearance of astral personalities. While your physical body is at rest, your true self journeys in the astral plane, or other dimensions. There, you exist in a more instinctual way, manifesting the true quality of your self and generally settling old scores with others and life. However you might also use the ability to travel into spiritual dimensions in a positive way, for instance to heal your karma, meet other individuals - human or not- attend classes, or even, when you are ready, interplanetary councils.

The student must be aware of these non-integrated parts of himself, in order for him to purify his shadow, and to stop building karma for the future. In doing so, the apprentice will not only prepare himself for the next steps on the path toward initiation, but also participate in the purification of the aura of the planet and thus the spiritual evolution of the Logos.

- Finally, a human being is much more sophisticated than you would

140

normally believe. In fact, he is one of the expansions or manifestations of a multi-dimensional Whole. The soul and the Monad express themselves at the same time under various disguises, on several dimensions and in numerous places. The development of the Consciousness is the means in which to connect with these other parts of the self, in order to experience them and then integrate them. The evolution of the human race will take place with the opening of the unconscious faculties, the so called para-normal ones, and the ability for each of us to live beyond space and time, in order to merge with the life of the Logoi, of the Universes, of God. It is the awareness of being part of this Whole, of the Absolute, the constant exchange of substance and intent, that will create and nourish universal Love and generate boundless peace.

Given below is a basic technique that you might use during your healing process on multi-personality, whether human or extra dimensional.

EXERCISE

- RECONNECTING WITH THE SUB-PERSONALITIES

- Be comfortably seated. Take deep breaths.

- Call your soul or Higher self and merge with it.

- Have your sub-personality appear in front of you — a little girl or young boy, liar, thief, Mr. Doubt, Mr. Self Sabotage...

- Tell him (or her) that you love him, that you understand his reactions. Explain that you know he is doing his best, in the spirit of helping you. Nevertheless, in order for you both to be happier in the present and the future, you have to work together. Tell him that he will be protected, but that you, as

141

the Higher Self, are willing to take control of your life.
-Visualize a cord or ray of Light, connecting your solar, heart, frontal chakras, with those of your sub-personality. Feel how a link between the two is now forming.

- Visualize and feel the Light increasing and surrounding you totally, including this part/these parts of you. Merge this sub-personality with your Higher Self.

- Give Thanks.

3. KARMA

Karma is generally defined as the law of cause and effect, as the result of past actions or events. In this chapter we would like to look at the problem of karma from a slightly different, more technical angle. We will speak about the structure of energy, karma as the consequence of your thoughts and interactions with forces, individuals and groups.

"In fact, it is not karma that rewards or punishes, but ourselves; we are the ones who reward or punish, depending upon whether we work with, according to and in agreement with nature, in remaining faithful to the laws that create Harmony or in failing to comply with these laws." H.P. Blavatsky, Secret Doctrine.

You live within matter in order to experience a range of specific vibrations and then to balance and harmonize your reactions to these outside frequencies, materialized through situations or specific people. The ultimate goal of these adventures is to be able to experience your own personal note, within both intimate and universal awareness, in total freedom. Freedom is a situation of non-suffering, of joy, proceeding from the regained capacity to live without conflict: this does not mean that any antagonism has been suppressed, but that it has been resolved and integrated. Then the soul is able to express itself in dancing, in a harmonious wave, without any sense of shock.

Your KARMA, the obstacles or avenues that are offered to you in your life, are the MATERIALIZATION OF THE FREQUENCIES that you are sending out. How were these frequencies built up?

1. COMING INTO INCARNATION AND KARMA

The human species has been shaped by its journey within precise cycles of evolution that have culminated in man/woman as you know them. During their trajectory, the souls, incarnated down here have been subjected to multiple factors of vibratory modulation:

- The Divine Vibration, originating from the Whole, from Love.
- The vibration of the Separation, the abandonment by the Whole, the individualization.
- The vibration of the planet and the planetary Logos, of which you are an integral part.
- The possible incarnations in other systems, for a precise group of souls.
- The external or astral influences, the sending out of energies from other intergalactic civilizations or spiritual groups.
- The family or group of souls with which you share specific interests and a karma.
- The beings, groups, energy masses that you meet life after life.
- The energies that you are building up according to your vibratory state and level of consciousness, which are a reflection of your deepest thoughts.

Separation has inevitably marked each one of you as a shock. Although individualization is a much tougher initiation than your birth on the planet, we will use this as an example to describe your sensations.

You live in a warm and cozy cocoon, you literally belong to another body whose genetic make-up, whose essence are also yours. This loving body brings you protection, strength, food, sometimes ups and downs, sometimes it is also screaming with anger. But this being who carries you is there for you, in fact *is* you. An almost complete symbiosis exists between these two souls, these two bodies; the two do not yet fully exist. This exchange is based on love, it is love. And suddenly, through suffering, you lose everything. You are alone, abandoned. You have to learn to exist, breathe, feed yourself, cry out to call someone, explore space. When you start moving, you run into an obstacle, matter. You have to submit to physical laws — for instance, you might fall and hurt yourself. You have to sleep, digest, eliminate waste, deal with unknown presences, whether friendly or hostile.

Imagine then the frustration you felt when you left the All in One. From the beginning of your experience, you have been subjected to a dissonance, a distortion of the frequencies that are your true self.

2. PARTICIPATION IN THE PLANETARY KARMA

Ever since you first established yourself on Earth, you have been taking part in the breathing of the One who maintains, through his presence, through his will and love, the spiritual body of the planet. We are speaking of the planetary entity of which you are a member.

This logos, itself intimately united to a larger spiritual body connected to a system of chakras and a specific vibratory ray, is a manifestation, a combination of these factors and frequencies. Although radiant, extremely evolved, the planetary Logos assumes and spreads its own karma. The logos has accepted situations in which he makes and will make choices, according to his distinct spiritual trajectory and to the influences and decisions of the spiritual hierarchies.

Through your Logos, you are evolving towards the vibration of Love-Wisdom. Please note that the Sanat Kumara who vitalized the frequency of thought, the mind, also came from the planet Venus. Venus is a symbol of Love but, also, it is sometimes named Lucifer. "Pythagoras called Sukra-Venus the Sol alter, 'the other sun.' On the 'seven palaces of the Sun,' that of Lucifer Venus is the third one in Christian and Jewish Kabala... Venus-Lucifer, the occult sister and alter-ego of the Earth." H.P. Blavatsky, *Secret Doctrine.* Sanat Kumara is then involved in a mysterious way with the Energy/Karma emanating from this planet.

3. YOUR LINKS WITH NEIGHBORING PLANETS

After the Separation, some people went through multiple adventures in other galaxies and planets. Their frequencies were then impregnated by these systems, their way of living, the education they received there. It is also probable, on the subtle planes, that these individuals have kept up relationships with their spiritual families. A number of them choose to participate in the terrestrial experiment, in order to have more irons in the fire, as it were, or to help humankind in its evolution. Finally, some of you are down here with a desire for domination, for infiltration of the planet.

Well, here you are now on planet Earth. Humankind initiates a mode of existence based on the first chakra. People live with instinct, the force, a still fresh contact with the spiritual realms, as well as with the very concrete power of the terrestrial substance.

You have to learn how to survive in a jungle, surrounded by fantastic animals, on a planet that is young and very much alive. We are far from feeling like a baby just emerging from our mother's womb!

Each one of you has been adjusting according to your personal note, although it has already been distorted by the influences mentioned above. You invent a form of existence in order to live or survive in these conditions, whatever they are. Laws, a morality, are created to support and follow the groups that arise, and then societies. These rules, a reflection of those who momentarily wield power, suit you or frustrate you, and you use them to build your belief system, your subconscious matter, your karma.

Imagine, for instance, that faced with some act of brutality, you

146

would have to surrender. This experience gives rise to anger and pain. On a more subtle level, the frequency of your soul is subjected to a tension that will create an imbalance if not released. This inharmonious vibration might then be recorded in your memories, your genetic codes. You will then attract and magnetize situations and beings that vibrate on the same frequency. Although this interferes with the pure note of your divine spark, you must then confront, as a mirror effect, in others, the discordant vibration that is now within you.

How many events, people, auras have been interfering in your energy shield since the beginning of time?

KARMA IS THE SUM OF THE ENERGY PATTERNS CREATED BY YOUR INTERACTIONS WITH INDIVIDUALS, GROUPS, SPIRITUAL HIERARCHIES.

1. YOU ARE ESSENTIALLY AN ENERGY that is manifested through a physical vehicle and subtle bodies. Your terrestrial vehicle is the concretization of a note, a sound, a color. Your soul has attracted, modulated a physical envelope that corresponds to these frequencies. This body functions in connection with the subtle envelopes whose most aggressive part, beyond any doubt is the astral or emotional body. As its name suggests, the latter is an expression of your emotions.

2. YOU ARE CONSTANTLY SENDING OUT VIBRATIONS with your mind - projecting what you are, intrinsically, as a spiritual force - your mind/thoughts, your subconscious mind or memory record. These waves, as thought forms, modify your subtle bodies.

3. By the contact of the auras, any MEETING OR

INTERFERENCE affects your subtle matter. You then modify your magnetic field by your emotional re-actions, colored by your subconscious mind.

4. You encounter DIFFICULTIES any time a situation goes against your desires or intimate sensations, against your education and system of beliefs. If you have to act in a way that is in contradiction to your thoughts, your soul-personality, the incongruence, the incoherence, the disharmony, will create a disequilibrium, a sickness of the soul and the body. Your vibrations will then be based on uncertainty, resentment, anger, anxiety or any other destructive emotion. This dis-ease will then be the basis for a DISTORTION of your ETHERIC MATTER, of the constitution of your whole self, of your karma.

To make things a little more complicated, or more exciting - it is just a question of point of view - some GROUPS of individuals have developed special relationships. For instance, you might have had a key role with the Cathars and be back, from incarnation to incarnation, with your companions, in order to join them in pursuing a specific mission. The beings who, consciously or not, participated in dramas or turning points in history, share a group karma, positive or negative, a similar vibration. It is then obvious that their karmas will be connected and that invisible forces will push them into common situations. This will continue up until the time they will have finished their task or will have evolved together.

On this subject, it is fascinating to retrace the history of some political world figures, or of the members of a family, through the use of inter-dimensional travel, past/parallel lives, or astrology. These combined forces create the magnetic and physical environment, the future, the beings and events that you are and will be attracting. According to the depth and strength of the frequencies sent out, you create a karma, and it will be concretized immediately or in a future incarnation.

KARMA IS THE SUM OF
THE ENERGY MASSES AND LINKS
THAT ARE BUILT BETWEEN YOU AND OTHERS.

Whenever a being has reached emotional maturity and stability, when his personality has been developed and integrated, his subtle bodies are clear, strong and consistent. This means that he is no longer affected by the presence of others. His relationships take place in harmony, without any friction.

But before reaching such a state, during your terrestrial journey you meet countless individuals. Some of them attract you, with others you feel an immediate dislike. An exchange of energy is established between you and the other person, materialized on the subtle bodies as a link, a tie that binds you. What is more, your physical vehicle will bear the mark, the imprint of this etherical matter. It is one of the manifestations of cellular memory.

Let us take the example of any relationship with a friend. At the beginning of the relationship, you establish a contact based on the fact that you like each other. Your cardiac chakras are communicating. You talk with this friend often and your conversations are materialized by a rope between your throat centers. A little later, your relationship becomes an intimate one and a bridge is built between the number two chakras. And if, in the final analysis, you end up fighting against each other, your chakras number three will definitely come into play.

We have exaggerated this example at bit, but let us say that individuals are connected by the chakra that deals with the main purpose of their encounter. Thus, if the lesson is to understand or to stop a controlling relationship, the 3rd chakra is then involved.

149

Whenever two persons have a partnership that is essentially based on sexuality, the link will, of course, be rooted in the second chakra.

When your contacts with others are more superficial, you might be keeping a memory of this meeting on points on your body that are not as strategic as the chakras. These areas will eventually be revealed to you when getting a massage or energy healing. As soon as the practitioner applies his hand on the muscle, a thought, an image immediately rises up in your mind, an emotion overwhelms you. It is the remembering recorded within your cells, the vibratory mark of your meeting, of any feelings created and recorded on your body.

These memories engraved in your cells, the links connecting your chakras to others are the masses of energy that determine the quality of your global frequency, the shape of your physical structure, YOUR KARMA.

Let us keep in mind that the physical form is a mass of energies, held together according to a code of information. Your karma, with which you are born, is the basic program. Then, the thoughts and frequencies that you take on are the data that you keep adding to this program. This means that you are responsible for the quality of the information that you input into your personal computer. Also, this implies that you have the ability to change your physical form and the life or belief system in which you choose to evolve.

HOW TO GET RID OF YOUR KARMA?

The universe obeys laws, some of which are immutable. The terrestrial principles are essentially based on the ongoing exchanges between Matter and Spirit.

EXPERIENCING THE VIBRATION OF YOUR SOUL
First, again and always, in changing your level of vibration.

Standing as close as possible to the innate frequency of your soul, in order to erase any discrepancy between your real note and the life that you are living.

In order to accomplish this successfully, you must:

- Learn to know your soul. Using meditation and daily contact, you will get to know her, this soul of yours, more deeply and with more clarity. You will develop a close relationship up until the time when you will become your own soul.

- Know yourself intimately, having persistence and courage in discovering your human personality. It is drama vs. divine purity. The revelation of your own personality will make possible a reconstruction, and then a stabilization of your self, according to your own needs and perceptions. Thus, you will become not only stronger but also more enlightened.

Any spiritual work implies a change and an internal reprogramming; however, the final key is to accept yourself, with your own strength and weakness, as a piece, a helpful cog in the humongous wheel of the universe.

- Free yourself from anything you have learned from your family or religion that does not fit with your true self, and then

151

live according to your transcendent awareness.

The true spiritual path is the one of pure truth. No group, no master, book, system of philosophy or religion is necessary. All these are but tools presented to you at a precise moment in your life to remind you of a forgotten truth - a reality that fits only you and only at that moment. To bind yourself would be to give yourself limits.

- Join the group, the society in which you live, in a way that does not alter your spiritual understanding and your intimate vibration. The ability to live in peace, detachment, without the need for fighting, always reacting to others and external events without having to prove that you are right, the art of floating on top of the wave, will put a end to the formation of your karma.

- Detach yourself from any personal relationship that is destroying you or bringing you out of balance; or even better, be balanced within your own energy to such a degree that you will not be affected by the energy or thoughts of other people and will no longer attract the frequencies that are hostile to your own soul.

A PRACTICAL POINT OF VIEW

We will give you practical techniques that will allow you to cleanse your karma, from the standpoint of purification, the revitalization of your subtle bodies. But once again we will insist on the necessity of carrying out your internal rejuvenation at the same time. Working on the personality and on communication with the soul are and will remain the basis for reintegration.

If we admit that our relationships with others create bonds, energy cords and impressions - remember that the word "impression" comes from the verb "to imprint" - on your triple body, you can easily imagine that it is possible for you to cut these links, to erase the prints left by your encounters with the exterior world.

EXERCISES

1. ELIMINATION OF KARMA. GLOBAL TECHNIQUE.

- Be seated in a lotus position or on a chair, between 3 white candles.
- Call forth the presence of your guardian angels, your guides.
- Relax and take 7 deep breaths to relax your body even more and to free you from your daily worries.
- Say out loud that you intend to release your karma, and then ask the Masters for their assistance.

For instance:

"As a soul and as a human being, I ..., request the assistance of the Masters of Light, of the Sanat Kumara and the Lords of Karma, in order to free myself from part of my karma. In doing so, I realize that I am taking part in the general evolution of human-kind and the freeing of karma that the Sanat Kumara and the planet took charge of."

- Inhale deeply, visualizing the Light enter into you through the top of your head (crown chakra).
- Exhale, visualizing the Light going through your body and cleansing it. Let any residue fall to the ground. If any images or impressions happen to come into to your consciousness, accept them.

Practice for 15 minutes. This technique might be used once or twice a week. Your intuition will let you know when it would be a good time to concentrate on this practice.

2. DEPROGRAMMING YOUR BODY OF AN EMOTION, A SHOCK

- Be seated, take deep breaths, relax.

- Choose a spot on your body that often manifests an illness or pain.

- Focus your attention on this area. Do you feel pain? Any heaviness? If necessary, place your left hand on the organ, the muscle, the joint, etc...

- Ask your Higher Self, your Soul, what it is that causes your pain, the dis-ease that you are feeling.

- Close your eyes and let the images, words, persons come to you. Surrender to the sensations, the emotions related to these individuals and/or situations; then let them go off into the Light.

- If necessary, put the persons or situations into the Light in order to transmute your feelings and those of others. Or, while visualizing, change the framework of the story in a way that is positive and supportive. A metamorphosis of the emotions will create new internal programs.

- You can purify your aura in imagining a thick, gray layer of toxins that is leaving your body, or a Band-Aid that you re move from your skin. Finish up by applying a luminous strip onto the wound.

- If you feel like it, move on to another strategic area of your body. Do this exercise again.

154

3. CUTTING YOUR RELATIONSHIPS WITH SOMEONE ELSE, EITHER HUMAN OR EXTRA-HUMAN, ACTUALLY ALIVE OR AROUND YOU.

Some persons that you have met in this or another dimension might have a harmful effect on your present life, and they pollute your frequency. You can, in all integrity, and in keeping with a conscious decision, decide to cut your ties to this person.

Nevertheless, before you do this, you will have to have understood and resolved, as much as possible, the reasons for your joint karma. No one has to be subject to the influence of another person if he does not want this to happen, consciously or subconsciously, or has not finished a specific contract in this regard.

- Be seated, in your usual working or meditating position.

- Lay out 3 candles, preferably white, as a triangle.

- Visualize as sitting in front of you the person you need to 'work out a situation' with.

- Call out to him, using his name, even saying it out loud.

- Explain the situation to him clearly, tell him how your hostile relationship or lack of understanding is hurting you both, on both a human and spiritual level. Let him know that you want the circumstances to evolve toward peace and your mutual enlightenment.

Two solutions will then appear:

1. Your interlocutor will be willing to solve the problem and a

dialogue will begin. You can re-write your story, or rather, it will take shape before your eyes, as a vision (creative imagery), with an outcome that is positive and enriching for both parties.

2. He refuses to negotiate. It is then your duty to tell him that you are willing to end all communications with him, and thus free yourself from a burdening karma.

Visualize the ties that bind you to each other as a white cord, coiled around your two bodies.

- Out loud, explain to your interlocutor what you are going to do. If you feel like it, you might even tell him why.

- Still out loud, repeat: "With this ritual and through this gesture, I hereby break apart and destroy any physical, emotional, astral and spiritual links that might exist between me and ..., in the past, present and the future. So be it, in the name of the Light, in Unconditional Love."

- Visualize then a big pair of scissors that cut the white cord. The pieces of the cord dissolve and are recycled into particles of Light.

- Watch the other person stand up, turn his back to you and walk into the distance and blend in with the landscape.

- Give Thanks.
  Excerpt from "Satanic Ritual Abuse and Spirituality."

* * *

In conclusion, we would like to guide you a little further in your reasoning about karma. Karma is the response created by the presence of two opposing forces. Once again we are dealing with duality. Form exists by bringing the reaction of two antagonistic energies face to face, energies that we might call positive and negative. The Universes themselves were brought to life by the reproduction, the duplication of the Universal Spirit.

Therefore it is impossible to experience matter and form without karma. The abolition of the karma implies the conclusion of life into form, the negation of the atom, which is in itself an aggregate of antagonistic forces. The suppression of the law of karma is the return to the Spirit or Universal Consciousness.

SECTION FOUR: THE DISCIPLE'S LIFE ALONG THE PATH

1. MEDITATION - IN SEARCH OF I AM

Meditation has always been considered to be the supreme way. Whenever it is practiced in accordance with the Hindu techniques, brought about by the dance of the Sufi or adapted for Christian prayers, the goal is the same - to let go of your thoughts in order to return to BEING.

You have been brought up to engage in thought, to put everything down in equations, in logical patterns. You have purged your societies and your heart of a process of daily contemplation, the state of BEING, in silence and reverence.

No one ever stops to smell the roses anymore; people merely look at things critically and attribute them a price.

No one ever stops to admire the roses, to lose oneself in their perfume. Instead, one evaluates, attributes a price.

Every day, give yourself over to your heart, to the child dormant within you, to the angel watching over you, a moment of peace without any questions. Then, you will discover BEING.

No more thinking, no more setting up your mental scaffolding built of whys and wherefores, of how and how much. How wonderful this would be, you say. But, this is indeed possible from that moment on when you decide to give up subjugating yourself to the impossible games of your mind.

You have become accustomed to confusing the action of thought with the fact of existence; we have even confused these two words *note.

It is the inherited Spirit, this treasure within you, that you want to regain when you meditate. You put an end to confusion, to illusion; you forget to think, to use your brain as a totalitarian and sometimes even Machiavellian computer. And, in Silence, you find your way back to Spirit.

You are no longer in the process of speaking, thinking, doing, you simply ARE. "I AM THAT I AM". You have found your way back to God, to Source.

Within you, in silent prayer, a prayer without words, without expression or reasoning, you have broken through the veil and are contemplating the strength, the beauty of... I Am.

God does not need to speak to express Himself, to make Himself known; he simply needs to BE.

God does not need to move or dance frenetically in order to hold the entire universe in His breath; His presence ALONE is enough.

God does not need to ask, to anticipate or regret in order to create because everything simply IS -beyond time, contained, beyond doubts, solely within His presence.

You ARE, UNIQUE. EVERYTHING YOU NEED IS WITHIN YOU, is innate in you.

Note: (in French, both "mind" and "spirit" are actually "spirit", "esprit". Fortunately we can use a capital letter to designate the Spirit that comes from God, this part of the divine that is in us, which we have inherited, which has been bequeathed to us for our great adventure here on Earth, in matter).

You simply need to know this, to return to Source. Then, knowledge, peace, joy and abundance will be within reach to you.

But, do we even *need* words? Because, as soon as we claim for more awareness, more rest, more blessings, we separate ourselves from Silence, from Source.

However, this is our nature, we humans, as participants in the nature of physical beings. As such, it is our duty to be familiar with the processes of thought, with analytical thought, as well as to build, destroy and understand the mechanisms of life, in order for us to leave all this and return to Source.

Christ sanctified the bread, consecrated his body, in carrying out his mission on Earth. He then gave rise to the re-union with the Spirit. It is the glorified Christ, whose spirit conquered matter, whom you meet, whom you *rejoin* when you experience the baptism of Spirit, when the subatomic vibrations of the Light have transformed your innermost nature.

Find a time, each and every day, to sit, to MEDITATE. Here, we do not mean any work with your mind or thoughts, with visualization, with travel through time and space, with questions raised. No, go to the center, the place where the nucleus of the soul resides, your heart. You can bring to it a pink ray, the ray of Unconditional Love. After that, forget everything else - words, other people, yourself, even your breathing. You NO LONGER THINK, you ARE.

"I AM"

The warmth, gentleness, grandeur, beauty, the colors of the BEINGNESS will then be revealed to you.

The longer you spend in this timeless space, the more you will heal any scars inherent in your life as it exists in matter, the more your body will become accustomed to and even seek out this state; the more the Spirit will inundate your cells until they are changed, transmuted. Until the time of Transfiguration.

Without any doubt, meditation is the most reliable method, the most spiritual, if I dare say so, to free you from all your questions, your apprehension, your karma, to transform your deepest nature, through daily contact with God; through revelation, the intimate certitude of the Kingdom within you. I AM. JE SUIS.

We can never repeat this often enough. Make this daily practice be your joy, your support, your friend. Do this in the morning, in order to illuminate your day, to consecrate it; in the evening, in order to find peace, to guide your nocturnal travels. MEDITATE, at least 20 minutes, twice every day.

At the beginning, this might seem to be just an exercise, even a kind of sacrifice; but very soon, you will find that you have come to need it.

The communication with GOD, I AM, is one of the most important, precious moment of the day. This is also a rejuvenating experience, bath in the Fountain of Youth*, the restoration of the supremacy of the soul, the recognition of its position as the captain of the boat.

"GOD WITHIN ME, ME, I AM"

Jouvence, in French.

MAJOR INITIATIONS

The word INITIATION is used in most esoteric schools to designate a passage, a renewal of consciousness, a step toward evolution.

True initiations are those that are organized and conducted by the Spiritual Hierarchy of your own system. They occur simultaneously on the physical, astral and spiritual planes of existence. If the student does not always remember going through the first initiations, nevertheless he will usually remember the ones that follow.

Although the primary initiations are the same for all of us, they are however personalized and modulated by the individual and planetary karma. Each person will experience them at his own pace, in his own way. The effect of the initiations is not always and immediately obvious, nor is it felt on the physical plane. For instance, although the health of the disciples is stabilized, they do not become perfect and insensitive to bacteria from one day to the next. They are not necessarily capable of materializing like Sai Baba in India. There is a time of adaptation, when deep changes take place, in the physical body, at a molecular level, in order for the being, under the limitations of his karmic agreements, to be able to manifest the effects of the initiation on the physical plane.

It is quite difficult to describe the Initiation process. We would advise you to study the works of Alice Bailey about this vast subject. At any rate, you are experiencing a period in history in which thousand of individuals are receiving the third through the sixth initiations, in what we would call an accelerated manner. This is the result of specific vibrational planetary influences, as well as of the evolution of the spiritual entities who are dominating your lives, and the will of the planetary and solar Hierarchies. The evolution and initiation cycles are divided by 7. The systems, the globes, the Hierarchies move up the levels of spiritualization going through 7 successive cycles, and continue to do so up to the infinite or Absolute.

The first four initiations are the base, the construction in the world of the form and matter. In human terms, this is the time for the development and the comprehension inherent to the four first centers/chakras and planes of existence. The three next levels are spiritual ones.

Thus, in the course of his path on earth, the disciple will be given **7 primary initiations,** during which the being passes through the Hall of Ignorance, then the Hall of Knowledge, and finally the Hall of Wisdom. These initiations occur and connect with the seven sub-planes that form the terrestrial realm, the level that all human beings must assimilate and overcome.

The **first initiation** concerns the awareness of living in the body, the mastery of the physical plane. The being discovers who he is, what existence means, just like at the moment of physical birth, but he is now being born spiritually, in and by the body. He has the intuition of the presence of his Angel, of an active intelligence that has made his life within the body possible but that is the real self. The first challenge/test is then to master the most basic passions and to set out on the path of control of the physical self, in order to purify it and to make it a more appropriate vase for the arrival of the solar Angel.

The Christ endured this state when he was born in a physical body. He, then, is the one who officiates during the ceremony, He who touches the cardiac chakra. The principal of life stored in the first chakra is recognized and vitalized by the future energy of the human race — energy that is spiritual, cardiac and christic. The **second initiation** is related to the control of the desires and emotions and the control of the astral plane and body. This can be a long and difficult period of crises and loss of the self in the area of illusion and the astral forms.

The initiate experiences the Presence from the standpoint angle of Duality; he realizes that the active intelligence aspect must be harmonized by the love/wisdom, which, in fact, is the origin of everything.

Christ is the Hierophant and stimulates the throat chakra. Desires, on the human plane, are connected primarily to the flesh, the need for mating, the second chakra. During the second initiation, this center is spiritualized by the creative vibration of the throat chakra.

When the disciple passes the **third initiation,** he will have mastered the mental plane. His mind is now sufficiently strong and organized; he is then capable of creating though forms. He is also acquiring more knowledge and acquiring it faster.

The initiate recognizes and integrates this fact that his real self is triple, because the fires of intelligence and of love unite in the accomplishment of a unique purpose, and create the Will Energy/Fire.

This initiation signals the contact with the soul and the Lord of the World, the Sanat Kumara. The centers of the head are vitalized.

The **fourth initiation** is called the Renunciation or Crucifixion. The human being has mastered matter, the personality, represented by the three lower chakras and has merged with the Monad. The causal body, built on the harmonization of the 3 permanent atoms, no longer has any reason to exist and is consumed by fire. The Solar Angel has played his role by means of the physical, astral and causal vehicles. He then withdraws in order to make way for the pure divine essence, the Monad.

In order for him to reach the higher centers — the throat, forehead, crown of the head — the student must advance through the middle of the cross, into the heart. He achieves the union of Spirit and Matter. He renounces everything, including himself, his own personality. His sole guide becomes the Monad, his Divine essence, for which his feels the Love aspect.

For the **fifth initiation,** the initiate has coordinated and mastered the Buddhic plane and will participate more intimately in the unity. "When the latent fire of the personality or lower self blends with the fire of the mind, that of the higher self, and finally merges with the Divine Flame, that is when man passes the fifth initiation in this solar system." Treatise of Cosmic Fire. Alice Bailey.

During the initiation, he receives, at least at times, the vision, the grasping of his belonging to the Whole. In the future, as a Monad, he will keep this imprinted memory and will feel integrated into the body of the Logos, in the triple energy of the system to which he belongs. Working in closest possible communication with the Great Lodge, he, in turn, puts together a group that he works with and that he teaches, on the subtle and physical planes.

The **six initiation,** also called Ascension, is one of the specific goals that humankind is to accomplish in the 1990s. The doors are already open and the Lodge stands ready to help you. The Disciple must have mastered the three worlds. To do so, he has connected the three permanent atoms and cleansed the central channel or shushuma to allow the energy of the Kundalini to arise.

165

He has built the bridge of Antakaranah and connected it to the Monad and to the Hierarchies.

He is detached from this world, whether or not he decides to stay in incarnation. His primary purpose is service, in close collaboration with Shamballa; his energy becomes stronger and stronger and is perceived by the students, the group with which he is working.

The bud of the lotus is opened and the secret of Buddha is revealed. Although he has parted with most of his karma, the Disciple understands in the deepest possible way the nature of the karma of the planetary Logos and assists in its transmutation. The Logos will move on to a higher plane when a sufficient number of human beings have reached the stage of Ascension or Illumination.

After the **Seventh initiation,** the Disciple, released from the physical world, from the 7 planetary planes, now functions as a whole within the Whole. He is no longer limited to the solar system. His incarnation is of a voluntary nature. His Monad has been reunited with the group or family that it belongs to and has merged with it.

THE SOUL MERGE
Or Marriage with the Soul

"Master? What is that, a Master? And anyway, I hate gurus!"

But this book by Yogananda well, it just seems right. It is simple, direct, true. I like his personality - I like his Master too, Sri Yukteswar.

They talk about meditation, about the Himalayas. That's so far away, and yet...

Here I am, in the middle of the mountains. It is a bit dry, invigorating, not at all cold. But then do you feel cold if you are projected out of your body? To be precise, I do not use astral travel, but rather travel on the mental plane. It's quick and easy.

The Master is teaching a small group of students. I arrive on the scene in one fell swoop, a bit of a crash landing, and try, somewhat ludicrously, to sit in the lotus position just like the others. And, as in my physical shell, my knees resist. I force myself, grimacing as I do so, while the others laugh at me. Then I listen attentively and bathe with happiness in the spiritual aura of the group.

The next day I come back again, and I find that I am welcomed into the group with smiles and love. Suddenly, I am inundated with light, as if a rocket had just landed in my head. My whole body bursts open into colors and joy. All over me, a fantastic surge of energy is swirling around with supernatural sounds. All my chakras are being activated, they look like cascades of light and fire and their centers gleam. My aura, inordinately enlarged, shines. The light, the gold -I accept them, so happy now, and naive.

In this life time, I had forgotten all this, but when the fantastic returns, it seems so natural, like something that had been a part of me that has finally come back.

I have the sensation that the entire room is illuminated. Like a child, I taste the moment, although on an intellectual level I do not understand what is happening to me. I only know one thing - the joy and the Light.

When I decide to stand up, the experience fades away, but secretly, on the sly, I will remain in this aura for 3 days. All I have to do is close my eyes listen and everything comes back to me with an incredible strength. As soon as I find myself home alone, I sit down and the dance of the chakras begins all over again with a great power.

I continue to visit the Himalayas for several more weeks, then I move on to new experiences."

* * *

On the spiritual path, the Marriage with the Soul or 3rd initiation is a fundamental passage.

The candidate made his choice a long time ago. His life, dedicated to service, indeed often even to sacrifice, is completely focused on the REINTEGRATION INTO LIGHT.

He is familiar with his battles and sorrow here on Earth. He does not deny any of his characteristics, but will simply assume them and has thus resolved the problems inherent in Separation and Duality.

In his own flesh, he merged the extremes of the body, the passions, the hatred, and through this he has found an equilibrium. This stabilization of the personality, and then of tumultuous emotions came about, amongst other things, through the communication with I Am in the space of silence, in the heart.

The forces that are inherent in the terrestrial personality, seated and then mastered in the first three chakras, have been experienced, understood and then overcome.

He knows how and why he has been incarnated and centered firmly in his desire to live totally in his physical nature, without lying, without cheating.

The problems of procreation, the awareness and then mastery of

168

the masculine and feminine energy are neither a mystery nor an irrational force. For the disciple, it is the path toward Co-Creation in the restoration of I Am, the Creator, who will dwell in the 5th chakra.

The student knows who he is. He is aware of his power and does not relinquish it. He no longer has the need to fight or surrender in order to assert his presence. He likes and appreciates his own personality. He has now been able to center himself in the world, in the crowd, without getting lost, on the level of the 3rd chakra.

The disciple expresses his true essence, freely, using the throat center. He is ready to become a Creator, not only within the human kingdom but also with the material consecrated by the Spirit.

He has firmly establish the link to his intuition. Little by little, his spiritual vision develops, with discernment and wisdom.

The lotus is unfolding. After having progressed through the Halls of Ignorance/Knowledge and the Hall of Sacrifice, as well as passing through Love/Wisdom, the student now allows the petals of the bud to open, in order to welcome into himself the energy of the Buddha.

The Candidate is now ready to merge the forces of his Soul with those of his physical being, his personality. This fusion, this marriage takes place in the heart. The soul is finally stable to forge a path for itself in this purified vehicle, inhabited by a conscious personality that calls for this merging.

At times, the soul will reveal itself in an audible way, letting the disciple hear his own personal note. This sublime, pure sound is the manifestation of the soul; it comes from the higher planes

169

and is made accessible to the human ear. If you are lucky enough to hear your own note, keep it carefully stored in your memory. In the future, you will use this sound in your meditations. You will be immediately connected to God within you, and you will move directly on a higher plane.

I AM THAT I AM

The meeting with the BEING, the Divine within ourselves, in the present, is an essential step during the Disciple's life. However, this quotation, I AM THAT I AM, found in the Bible, is much more than mere words. The Word is a mantra, a force, especially when spoken in a sacred language.

The invisible Beings of the Hierarchy, who hold and sustain the solar and cosmic systems, use sounds in their meditation.

Imagine a gigantic council, an extraordinary circle of spiritual entities that meet in order to propel the race up to higher vibrations.

Any of these entities carries, within itself, in its body, a multitude of beings who are evolving at their own rhythm. Our Logos accepted the responsibility of a myriad of Consciousnesses that are the cells of his own body, YOU. By your own growth, you improve your capacity to sound the mantra that corresponds to your own level of consciousness. When a sufficient number of cells have attained Consciousness, our Logos will be able to rise up to another level along the path of Initiation.

I AM THAT I AM

IS THE MANTRA, THE EXPRESSION OF 3 LEVELS
OF INTEGRATION OF CONSCIOUSNESS

In Chapter 3, we mentioned the multiple structure of a human being. In fact, the being evolves not only by the internal, intrinsic change of the quality of his frequencies, but also, and most of all, by realization, by entering into AWARENESS.

I AM

is the awareness of individualization. The being has integrated the three kingdoms, animal, vegetable and mineral. He takes possession of a human body, secures for himself a place on a Globe - in your case, the planet Earth - and then discovers his personality. Using the human capacity for thought and discrimination, man is able to distinguish the self from the non-self. He identifies himself.

I AM THAT

The being has perfected himself through his personality. He has discovered his Ego and established the link with his soul. Freed from the lower planes, he begins to serve the Group; from here on, he lives in and for the body of the Hierarchy. The being has found his place in a chain.

I AM THAT I AM

Closer and closer to the spiritual planes, the Initiate realizes that, beyond the Soul, there is the Whole, the Spirit, of which he is a part. He has learned to differentiate between Matter, Soul and Spirit. His true self is, in fact, the Monad. Thus he frees himself from the manifestation and integrates himself into the System.

All the cells of the planetary Logos, and then of the Solar Logos must discover and then successfully integrate these 3 mantras or vibrations. This will occur as the result of the successive Initiations.

171

When enough cells have been purified and have become Light and Spirit, the whole body can go through a new initiation. This applies to the human being as well as to the Planet, the Logoi. Perfection, paradise are just terms to express the state that you may reach, in the Whole.

I AM A BEING OF LIGHT

Agni, Lord of Fire, Creator, Preserver and Destroyer, engenders the three fires that animate the human being. Agni is connected to the Sun. In order to be alive, the material body needs the rays of the physical sun. When man increases his emotions and Consciousness, he enters into resonance with the Heart of the Sun. Then, when he develops the Spiritual Will and functions on the plane of the Monad, the human being responds to the frequencies of the Spiritual Sun.

Light is the raw material used in all creation. In this chapter, we wish to make you aware of the necessity — whether or not your purification has been completed — of choosing and proclaiming your membership in the team of the Light and of integrating the Light within you.

Clearly, it is not by chance that you are reading this book. In this period that is crucial not only for your future but also for the future of the planet, the battle for supremacy becomes harder and harder. Not only are the forces of Light and the forces of the darkness engaged in ruthless combat, but the commandos of the neighboring systems are sending emissaries, preparing the crowds.

It is then simply recommended that you place yourself openly in the faction of the Light, that you use the strength and protection of the Universal Light in order to transmute the energy of power

172

into equilibrium. War is a disharmony, an exertion of the power of one camp over the other. Balance is the recognition of the Other, and the acceptance of the law of attraction/retraction. Sublimated and spiritualized, this law becomes the law of Love.

EXERCISE

You are in your bedroom or in front of your consecrated alter.

- Breathe deeply, relax.
- As much as possible, bring your mind to silence and put yourself into a state of meditation.
- State out loud that you belong to the Light:
  "As a soul and as a human being, I, ..., live and work, consciously and subconsciously, for the Universal Light.

On the human plane as well as in the multi-dimensional layers of my personality, I am a perfect channel for the Universal Light and Love."

- Visualize a column of Light, at least 3 feet in diameter, coming down from the sky, encompassing you and reaching the ground. Feel and consciously ask for the vitalization of your cells and chakras, of your DNA. Visualize the particles of light entering your cells, cleansing and activating the DNA.

- Now visualize four columns of light in the corners of your room, office, or wherever you are.

These columns are to be reactivated every day. After several weeks, you will have created a sanctuary in which you nurture, heal and metamorphose yourself with energy.

* * *

One of the keys for reintegration is service. Although the practice of visualization techniques is to be used as a tool of transformation, the understanding of your intimate self, the metamorphosis and service are the true foundations of your task.

This is the reason why one of the most efficient ways to become the Light is to work for the Light, to guide others to It.

We are not suggesting that you seek to gain converts, but rather that you carry the frequency of the Light. If you are radiating a certain vibration, if you are diffusing it around you, you will convey it to your interlocutors and drive them to different thoughts and then to change.

In a more direct manner, transmit the frequency of Light to others and you yourself will be the Light.

During your daily meditation:

- Surround the planet with a radiant, white bubble of Light. If you feel like it, you might send the Light to the areas affected by a war or natural disaster.

Personality	Matter	Human Body	I AM
Soul	Soul	Planetary Logos	I AM THAT
Monad	Spirit	Solar Logos	I AM THAT I AM

In doing so, you will be helping the Spiritual Hierarchies to re-balance and transmute the vibrations of the Earth.
- Depending upon your life style and circle of friends, send the radiations of the Light to the strategic points of your little world.

If every human being would spend only five minutes every morning working like this, the Earth would evolve much faster.

For instance, you might choose to wrap your children, your mate, their school or place of business in a bubble of light. That way you will bring them under the protection of the Hierarchies of the Light, and they will carry the vibratory message of the Light out into their daily environment.
- Send Light through your heart chakra to your close relations, friends, neighbors. You do not need to spend 10 minutes on each person. Nevertheless, give priority to anybody you are having problems with, those people who are making you angry. This will clear your path and decrease the amount of your karma.

Light is the raw, primordial Matter, infused by the Spirit or Cosmic Consciousness. It is the Mother.

The Spirit, superior abstract intelligence, does not have any form or appearance. The Spirit touches the Light and gives it direction and a vibratory orientation. A conductor of the Spirit, Light allows the Spirit to express itself.

The Light contains information dating back to the beginning of time. Anything the Light passes through will be infused with this information; the Light will also program things, people and systems. The Light moves through the Cosmos and perpetuates creation. Any obstacle in its way will generate a phenomenon of densification and then the formation of matter. All the colors of the spectrum, all the frequencies originate with the Light; you yourself are made out of densified Light, compressed into systems. By adding Consciousness you will initiate the converse movement, spiritualization.

2. MANIFESTED LOVE

A. SEXUALITY

Your body is the magic instrument that allows you to express your total Self; sexuality is the celebration of this receptacle of life and divine breath .

Sexuality is
  - A duplication of God's act of Creation.
  - An expression of the law of attraction
  - A connection to the Divine.

1. God, the original Consciousness, expressed Himself in the Reflection of the self. He extended Himself through space and created the microcosm. In the same way, all Life has a natural tendency to want to re-produce itself. Sexuality is one of the terrestrial methods of creation. God, in his infinite perfection, loves himself and thus reproduces Unconditional Love. The creature also gives life in the context of Love as well as expressing love by duplicating itself.

2. Although polarized by the sexes, the body conceals in its structures the two basic Energies, masculine and feminine. These two antagonistic and complementary forces are transmitted and genetically imprinted by:
  • Paternal and maternal heredity, karma.
  • The presence and attitude of the father and mother during your childhood.
  • Family and religious education.

Just like the Cosmos itself, human beings respond to the law of the attraction of opposites and then feel the need for wholeness,

176

for a balancing the energies. Therefore human beings will naturally look for a complement on Earth.

3. Sexual energy, one of the most powerful in the human system, can be used at different levels. Because man has not yet had access to all the power of the brain and the mind, he is using the power of Matter and Life coiled in the first chakras.

Bear in mind that this instinct for life has been given to you as a gift from the gods. And the gods, not without a sense of humor, give you — in the most primary expression of matter, at the moment that the masculine and feminine polarities merge — a magical moment in which you have a chance to meet them.

During orgasm, because of the opening of the energy centers and channels, you catch a glimpse of the feeling of beatitude created by the spiritual marriage. During this experience, although for most individuals it is far too short, you are given the opportunity to feel this unity — this oneness — and fusion, and to have access to what is Divine within you. Momentarily you are traveling on new states of consciousness. You are riding a moment of eternity in which your limitations can be abolished, not only through the power of the energies merging, but also through the adding of the vibration of Love. A window is opened, and you can either look out of it or jump from it, if you feel like it.

In the system of chakras, love and Creation reveal themselves on three different levels.

1. On the level of matter, in using the second and third centers. It is the purely sexual love, based on the discovery of the self, the development of self-esteem and self-love, the basic relationship with others.

2. When the being, more aware of and intimate with himself, has evolved, he will express love as a means of communication and an exchange of emotions and of energy, based on a synergy of the sexual, throat and cardiac chakras. The being is preparing himself for a phase of creation that is closest to the Divine. When he has purified the forces of his spirit and can express them, he will be a spiritual creator.

3. Having overcome, indeed mastered, the forces of matter, the Disciple activates the centers of the head. In touch with the Solar Angel, using the energy of the will, he reaches the mental plane and creates on the physical planes.

* * *

A number of religions, sects or gurus require from their disciples the practice of celibacy. Sometimes sanctions are imposed upon those who break the so-called divine law, and consciences are burdened by the weight of guilt.

The body responds to physical realities. You were created with a reproduction system, hormones and an etherical vehicle. Sexual physical desire is as normal as hunger, and the only way to change this is to modify your intimate energy structures. It is obvious that the student is encouraged to learn to control his physical urges, but a healthy sexual life is only the use of natural functions, which, when transmuted, will open the doors to the spiritual plane. Like certain monks, you can transfer the sexual energy in the cardiac and upper chakras. But the terrestrial system is still focused on the body through the lower centers. A time will come when you will have harmonized and stabilized your energies; your center of gravity will no more be the solar plexus, but the heart. You will no longer be at the mercy of your instincts and passions.

And of course you will no longer have the same physical reactions, the same way to consider relationships with others.

Whatever your stage of self-development, whatever your already have accomplished in the balancing of your energies, whether you have a need to express yourself sexually or simply do this by choice, as a participation in life or an expression of love, the sensual pleasures will be considered as a celebration and an art.

* * *

Numerous cults, connected to the use of the two first centers, include sexual rites. The vitalization of these chakras allows for a temporary contact with the powerful energy of Kundalini, of life; but also, in arousal and passion, man rediscovers his connection to the divine.

Kundalini, coiled in the first chakra, is the World Mother. She waits for the moment when the Father (pineal) is ready to attract her into his celestial home (Ajna).

Sexual intercourse stimulates the energy system
    • in activating the two first chakras
    • in furnishing the complementary energy, either male or female.
    • in vitalizing the hormonal and glandular system.

We ask that you consider sexuality under three different aspects.

1. The sexual act is an homage to the BODY and to BEAUTY.

Surrendering the self in the physical relationship, the being recognizes and accepts his animal nature. He consciously participates in the different stages of matter, while honoring his terrestrial vehicle.

In a moment of grace, he establishes a physical and sensuous

179

contact with his body. With your eyes, your sense of touch, you are celebrating a god made flesh.

Suddenly, physical form no longer has the same importance. Whatever your physical appearance, your age, the bodies — yours and your partner's — are ennobled, made more beautiful by the pleasure, the attraction produced by the senses or the presence of Love. Touch, creating pleasure and joy, then sculpt the form to give life to it.

Because women have a more intuitive contact with their body, as well as their emotions and a natural understanding of the beauty of the flesh, in the history of mankind they have often played the role of priestesses or instructors. In the Hindu tantric rites, the man and the woman personify the goddess Sakti and the god Shiva. The partners replay the drama of the cosmic marriage and participate in the beatitude created by the fusion, the Unity.

We recommend that you prepare for love as if for a hymn to beauty and HARMONY. A beautiful, clean, welcoming space, candles, the use of water and bathing as well as the scent of aromatic oils or incense — all this will certainly add to the charm and perfection of the romantic relationship.

Take time to admire, to demonstrate your love for the body, yours or your partner's, using your eyes. Greet your lover as the microcosmic representation of the Divine. A massage, maybe even with oils, in addition to its healing properties, is also a powerful message of tenderness, of self-surrender, of recognition of the other. The touch can be relaxing, nurturing, then sensuous. All the parts of the body have secrets to reveal; whether you are giving or receiving, forget about everyday things, your mind, and just surrender to your feelings.

2. This leads us to consider the sexual act as a MEANS of

COMMUNICATION. There are many impulses and outbursts of feelings that you do not know or cannot verbalize. The act of love, as we call it, is an open door to the expression not only of your feelings but also of your most intimate self. By an acceptance of fusing with the other, relinquishing for a moment your existence as a unique and separate entity, you have a taste of the divine expression of love, which is a relationship, cohesion, exchange.

Revealing yourself not only in your nakedness but also in the expression of your animal nature, is a proof of your trust, of your faith in yourself, in the greatness of physicality. It is a hymn to life. It is an acceptance of yourself, in your own body, a moment that your share and honor with the other.

You are communicating not only your desire or love for the other, love for your own body, but you are also recognizing in your lover a divine manifestation, in a vehicle of flesh, sometimes a mirror, a complement, an moment of grace in the human journey.

Kundalini is dormant in your first chakra. Keep in mind that this power is the sum total of who you are, as an energy and as a living being, with the memory of your past lives and information on everything you have learned or experienced in your inter-galactic travels.

At a cellular and energy level, the act of love opens you and then gives to your partner the opportunity to read and — at least unconsciously — to draw upon the memories and programming that you are unveiling. You may choose to give and receive the karmic and spiritual information imprinted in your cells and those of your partner. Of course, such an exchange, practiced by unaware beings, entails a number of risks. Having intercourse with an individual whose frequencies are too low or too dark, is a

181

burden that can debase you. Your aura, your spiritual bodies will suffer the consequences.

Conversely, if your partner is enlightened, happy, filled with understanding and a positive spiritual experience, any and all contact will increase your heritage and make your energy more attractive.

3. Finally, the act of love is a merging of energies. While you are sexually communicating with the other, you are building bridges between your chakras. You give and receive the vibrations of the other and integrate them into your own system.

Of course, through your meeting with a partner, you are awakening and connecting your masculine and feminine energies. As long as your own system has not been completed, by the building and balancing, within you, of the two frequencies, sexuality is a way to feel, literally to "decant" the missing energy from one recipient to the other.

It is also a trick that gives to your body an idea of the power and beauty created by the wholeness and balance of the energies. Under this impulse, your spiritual entity is giving you a model so that your might establish this reunification within yourself.

Using the third chakra, you connect to the level of the energy of control. You understand, then, the importance of your state of mind as well as that of your partner at the time you come together. If what is happening is not an exchange in understanding and in love, you are giving to an individual the right to surrender or submit to you. You are also weaving threads that will increase your karma. The sexual act could then be used as an exercise, teaching you how to take part without either controlling or giving yourself over in submission.

Of course, the fourth chakra will be nourished, vitalized, stimulated by the action of your partner's heart and by the energies that flow from the first centers.

Actually, we are simplifying the phenomenon quite a bit while explaining the connections that are building up between chakras, two by two. Try, instead, to imagine the sexual act as an instrument allowing you to plug in your own system, then to add to it a similar structure that will complement and nurture your own. In doing so, your energy system will be connected with more subtle frequencies, ones whose higher voltage will bring your frequency to a higher and stronger level.

Energy and spiritual communication through sexuality have been practiced all throughout history and in all parts of the world. You will probably hear about tantra. Although there is a purely sexual form of tantra, this word does not refer, as is often believed, to a specific form of sexuality, but rather to the art of communication with the energies, hidden within the body, in order to let these forces express themselves and evolve toward Oneness. Actually, it is a form of yoga.

"The word tantra means a knowledge of an experimental, systematic and scientific method that allows you to open your awareness and human faculties; it is a process through which the spiritual powers inherent in the individual take shape.

"The individual has an opportunity to achieve and bring himself into harmony with the Cosmic Awareness: to perceive this reality intuitively is the goal of tantra. The individual is not isolated, but rather integrated into the cosmic design." *The Tantric Way*. Ajit Mookerjee. Madhu Khanna.

When two persons practice sexual tantra, they are entering into a game that is of a cosmic nature, giving their relationship a new dimension and depth. They are no longer a man and a woman, enjoying the pleasures of the flesh, but rather God and Goddess, united in Love to perpetuate the meeting of the principles of male and female, the apotheosis of the universal marriage.

4. Many of you already use the act of love as a passage to other dimensions. As we have already said, sexual intercourse:
  - vitalizes the primordial energy, the chakras, the glands
  - puts you in communication with another frequency and all its heritage.
  - connects you to the energy of the planetary Logos and the divine vibration Love/Creation.

This is why you can use this intense moment to activate your spiritual and psychic faculties. Images will come to you about your past lives; you might be launched into other dimensions or visit neighboring galaxies, have visions come to you, or have access to spiritual information.

Finally, since sexuality is a hymn to matter and to the body, you might call your totem animal, in order to get used to its presence and to discover the key to call him back.

MARRIAGE

For a number of you, this is the functional and logical basis of the family unit. As a matter of fact, it is still difficult, within the current structures of our societies, to give our children, except within the framework of a marriage, parents and a model for developing their masculine and feminine energies. Also, the emotional growth of young human beings is still based on the perception of a stability due to the presence of both parents.

Nevertheless, our society is in the process of change. In the near future, children will no longer be raised in the same way. Consequently, our remarks about sexuality are not just limited to marriage or mating. Consenting adults have the right to activate their sexuality within the framework of various situations. Nowadays, there is an uncertainty that makes relationships between male and female more difficult than ever.

Man, the male, is discovering his emotions, intuition, sensitivity and his spiritual side. Progressively letting go of his position of dominance, of being a pillar of strength, he has a tendency, before balancing his energies, to dive into an extreme situation and to forget his masculinity or his responsibilities as a father.

Woman, the female, has stopped being a submissive and consenting being in order, instead, to experience strength and transcend her innate spirituality.

As a result, it proves to be difficult and sometimes humiliating for a man to lose his role as a warrior, with a weapon in his hand, in order to embrace his feminine and sensitive nature, especially if at the same time he must also compete with females who are actually learning combat!

As for the woman, aware that she is regaining the power, she is looking for a man who is capable of sensitivity and affection, but who does not see relationships as a means of control.

In short, current adjustments in your respective energies do not allow you to find the balanced partners that you are dreaming about. Therefore you have emotional lives that are often turbulent and force you to adapt constantly.

On a general basis, in unison with the planet Earth, you are gradually moving your energy center from the third to the fourth chakra. Woman ruled society during the evolution of the second center, and then man ruled society during the organization of the solar chakra. Both sexes are perfecting the stabilization of both male and female energies. When this process is completed, males and females will no longer be fighting for supremacy and will be expressing themselves through love - cardiac center.

While you are waiting for for such a blessed moment, we recommend that you select your partner with a great deal of care, so that this companion does not plunge you back into in the patterns of the past. In addition, your lover should not just be interested in stealing your energy, but should also honor you. Even if real love is not present, then at least express yourself in a deep feeling of respect for each other.

Of course, if you are fortunate enough to experience a relationship on the level of Love, your sexual exchange will be even more beautiful, harmonious and powerful.

IN THE BEDROOM

We have already discussed celebration; it is of course important to be spontaneous and completely natural. But sometimes you might want to initiate intimate relationships as a unique moment, a sacred act. You plan a special occasion and make time to love and honor your partner, in a spirit of respect. Consequently, we feel we must stress the importance of cleanliness, of an appropriate place to meet your partner, and even that you be resolute in selecting an aesthetic setting.

Keep in mind that your are going to celebrate, with a divine being, the dance of bodies and the merging of energies, Love. An inviting piece of fabric, a flower in a vase are enough to give an elegant, festive note to the ambiance. Your actions will intensify your intent and permeate the frequencies in which your meeting is taking place.

Light candles in the corners of the bedroom. Thus Light will be present, and will allow you to look at, admire, communicate with your partner, but it will also sculpt your bodies in a wonderful way.

Lay out crystals in the middle of or around the room, after programming them to help you vitalize the currents of energy - this is optional, although the results are very enticing! (Press the crystal against the ajna and send a message associated with energy; for example: "may our emotions be amplified many times over!")

Be seated in front of each other, possibly in a lotus position, and begin by communicating with your eyes and your voice.

It is not necessary to be sexual immediately. Give yourselves a moment of love, as an interlude away from your hectic everyday life. You probably have something that you want to talk about with your partner or a page that you would like to read together. If you are both on the path of awareness, this moment might be the ideal opportunity to speak about your last spiritual experiences or about your goals for the future.

If you are used to working with sounds, you may choose to change your frequencies, to increase the level of your energy by singing and toning together.

Get close enough to be able to join hands. Making eye contact - or keep your eyes closed if this will make it easier for you to feel - visualize vibratory bridges between your cardiac and sexual chakras. Feel the energy as it goes through your hands and your chakras.

Then, begin to establish a physical contact, sensual but not sexual. Touch your faces, your forearms, your feet. Lay your hand on your partner's forehead.

Establish a more concrete physical touch using massage or spiritual healing techniques. Let your hands move freely; they will probably discover the areas of tension on your lover's body and will comfort, relax and heal them.

Take the time to stop and just look at your partner, compliment him/her about the beauty of a given part of his/her body or about the gentleness of his/her massage. Each of you must in turn give and receive. Learn to receive, in trust and in surrender; this is all part of the game.

Do not forget to communicate through kissing, one of the most intimate connections with another person, especially since the mouth is a very important sensual and energy zone.

When you reach the point of a more sexual exchange, think of alternating periods of raw animal sex with moments of tenderness, of touching and of exercises in energy communication.

Whether or not there is a spontaneous outpouring of energy, take the time to feel the current flow between you and your partner and the opening of the chakras.

The act of love is not a quantitative performance. Instead of rushing to orgasm, as a goal to be achieved, let the waves of pleasure come over you, then relax, stop for a moment... Take advantage of the moment to express your feelings with words, activate more emotions, in fact the cardiac energy. An extended orgasm is possible if one slows down the process, in order for the entire body, the entire system to participate and slowly catch fire. Relaxation and breathing help you slow down ejaculation. The more you delay the pleasure, the stronger, the deeper the fireworks will be!

Certain positions are more appropriate for connecting the chakras. Learn to listen to your body and to feel when your centers react the most.

TECHNIQUE: CONNECTING AT
THE ENERGY LEVEL

- Visualize the energy of your first chakra as it rises along your spine, forms a circle, enters the top of your partner's head, and then finish the loop by coming back to you. Increase this flowing energy in a continuous movement, then activate the circle in the other direction.

- Your partner is working in the same way. In doing so, you activate your energy, flooding the higher centers, and share your frequency with your mate and receive his/her energy. While you are hugging, connect your foreheads to activate the Ajna and communicate through this center. This is called the tantric kiss.

In fact, whatever your moves or embraces might be, think about them as a yoga, a tool to communicate your love and share in terms of energy. Obviously, your chakras know what to do and how to move, your intent will activate them and soon you will be admiring their dance.

Usually your body moves because you impose upon it, with your mind, a certain direction. But if at times, finally, the energy over-

189

flows in your body to the point that it will guide you in the movement, simply surrender to this and contemplate.

B: THE LOVE CREATION VIBRATION

The human being holds within himself the seed of the Divine. He has the capacity to "be born into knowledge" (Co-Birth), to be united in full consciousness with Universal and Divine Love*. See page 114

Nevertheless, during the long pilgrimage into the kingdom of Maya, the pure frequency of the Creator's Love reaches us in a veiled way. The range of human sensations, although intense and sometimes innocent, is, for a long period of time only a pale reflection of Divine Love.

As a matter of fact, the student still has a tendency to restrict himself to the reflection, the emanation of his emotional body. The latter, as long as it is not stabilized and refined, creates emotions based on the ego, fear, the power struggle, outmoded patterns ingrained in the personal and collective subconscious.

For example, one of the facets of human love was built on the memory of one of the most dramatic religious pictures, the crucifixion, with the intense pain that that entails. People wear the cross around their neck, as a reminder of this painful situation, instead of focusing on the symbol of resurrection and reintegration. Divine Love is not crystallized in painful events, whether or not they existed as a reality, on the physical, subconscious or astral plane. Suffering and sorrow are not conditions necessary for the expression of Love. Joy, unselfish service, unconditional love are much more difficult to express in the relationship with others, the world, life, but of course, immensely constructive.

Human emotions are not based on the awareness of the spiritual

190

laws, but often on a narcissistic search for the self, in the other, as a conditional, a temporary emotion - the self evolves. You have a tendency to love what is similar to yourself, which could bring you a feeling of limited comfort. You do not see the other, outside your own self, for what he really is, but rather as the image that he projects, humanly and temporarily, on the veiled screen of your subconscious mind.

What is a DIVINE LOVE?

Start by reminding yourself, and reaffirming this, that because you are a recipient of the divine atom, anything that God is, owns, is also yours.

Divine love is based on conscious and integrated co-knowledge. It is the ability to love, whatever the circumstances or the object, without making judgments or asking questions, because God is far beyond judgment or problems.

The All in One contains in himself the totality of the frequencies, essences and capacities of manifestation. Manifesting himself, he has integrated the phenomenon of duplication and diversification into matter. This vibration comes back to Him in an eternal movement. It is the awareness of this movement, a participation in life that is projected, expressed and felt by the creation, which gives the Creator a total awareness and co-birth. Through this intimate participation, this complicity, the Whole cannot judge.

The All In One Is. The One communicates with all of creation, thinking or not. He communicates because He is indissoluble from creation, in the same way that creation cannot exist without him. The Spirit supports and animates creation, through his breath and presence. This intimate exchange is Love. It is the natural

ebb and flow of the Spirit between those two poles, between God and you, you and others, you and a flower, etc.
When you have reached this level of existence, without questioning, in the momentaneous and eternal state of Being, you will taste divine Love.

This Love, whose origin is in reflection and extension, is creative in its essence.

If you feel and remain in this Love frequency, you will be a Creator yourself.

It is then necessary to discover, re-initiate within yourself the love-creation vibration. Aligning yourself with this frequency, you will become your own creator. You will be able to extend yourself, manifest yourself. Your daily life cannot be a burden, but rather the expression of who you really are as a soul. This projection of your intimate self into matter is feasible as soon as you have fully integrated your divineness. No more questions will arise with regard to your sense of being accepted, to the self-love that you are able to feel, or to the image you have about yourself and the way you envision those who cross your path.

Just as the One loves in his participation in the Worlds, the Universes, the Atom, your love is an act of communication. It is the sharing, the becoming a part of the life around you and in the Other, giving him the right to be different and to express himself. Love is feeling what is physically outside the self as an extension, with whom there is an ebb and flow of energies, an osmosis.

Divine love, then, is a stream, flowing freely, without obstacles or hindrances; it is an exchange.

The Love-Creation vibration naturally finds its center in the cardiac chakra. The latter is capable of manifesting itself whenever the energies of the 3 lower chakras — which involve ignorance, fights, power, and a sexuality out of balance — have been understood and transcended, connected with the superior center — the Spirit. The heart is the point of equilibrium between the energies, on which you are willing to build your life, as the spiritual center of gravity.

Any questions of self-understanding, power, ego have been solved and possibly even integrated. The student is aware of the existence of his spiritual self and proceeds to build it step by step. He has taken his place in the Universe and in the Hierarchy of the planetary Masters. Each Master works on his own ray, while at the same time merging with the planetary ray, transmitted by the Sanat Kumara. The student must then carry out the mixing of the energy of his own ray with that of his direct Master. With his entire self he is in communication with the Hierarchy, using the cardiac vibration as the intermediary tool or support -Love-Communication-Osmosis.

In order to become Co-Creator, in his life or in collaboration with the spiritual Hierarchies, the initiate must have unburdened himself of any concepts or negative programs that might generate entropy and destruction. As we have already said, life is a perpetual equilibrium between the positive and negative poles, the creative and entropic/destructive forces. The Love/creation frequency, freed from the battle of the opposites and the obstacles of the subconscious mind, now stabilized, can concentrate and manifest itself.

FEELING COMMUNICATION WITH THE UNIVERSE

- Breathing and relaxation while sitting.

- Put your attention on your heart.

- Visualize a sphere of golden light in your cardiac chakra.

- Feel the warmth, the sweetness radiating from this spot. A vibration, a pulse is beating inside you, Emanation of the Divine Love. Feel this pulse. This energy, alive and spirited, spreads throughout your whole being. Feel this Love with all the fibers of you body.

- Then extend this sensation of love outside yourself, further and further, out of the room, reaching the whole planet, the edge of the Universe.

- At this point, this love vibration will come back to you, and little by little it will resume its place in your heart.

- Like at the center of a gigantic pulse, send this vibration back out, spread this vibration to the outside, and then receive it again. Keep yourself in tune with this pulse, indeed *become* the pulse, and then in silence, bathe yourself in the waves of Unconditional Love.

- Your heart is the organ of communication between you and the Universe. You are participating fully in the flow of the divine and creative Love.

- Come back slowly. Give Thanks.

194

3. WORKING ON THE CHAKRAS
AND THE ALTA MAJOR

INITIATION

The moon of Wesak is shining with all her strength, round and full. Happy, convinced the journey will be beautiful, I sit in a triangle of light and thank the Masters for their presence.

As soon as my eyes close, I find myself in Egypt, in the center of a secret room of the Great Pyramid, supported by the 12 Masters/ Brothers who have been with me since childhood. Around me, slightly hidden by the darkness, are the high priests.

TONIGHT, I AM TO MEET THE SERPENT.

Suddenly, I am alone, everyone has left, even my 12 Brothers. For an instant, my stomach is tight; the old, ancestral fear of the unknown dragon slips into me.

The Serpent, huge, climbs out of the ground, moves towards me, majestic, hieratic. We stare at each other, our eyes welded together.

Now, I have to enter his mouth, opened, dark.

I take a step and enter the abyss. Completely calm, without an ounce of fear, I penetrate the darkness. Then, as I am sliding further down, everything around me is suddenly illuminated, becomes Light. More exactly, I am diving down. I tumble through 7 circumvolutions, my whole body hurled forward by the movement. I think: "Matter, number 6, experienced 7 times. I complete a human cycle."

The Energy penetrates my skin, my bones. Two serpents are now intertwining in me, joining at the top of my head. Then, in a subtle, magical alchemy, I become, I *am* the Serpent.

Back in the initiation room, the priests place me in a tomb. I am not afraid, just cold. Thirty-six hours in the tomb are required, as a symbolic death, which I experience deeply, serenely, almost with delight.

When I emerge from the tomb, the priests greet me. They tie my hands firmly behind my back and MENTALLY BREAK MY LINK WITH THE SPIRITUAL KINGDOMS, THE LINK ON THE BACK OF MY NECK, ON THE ALTA MAJOR. Then they throw me out into the burning desert, with these words:

"You must find the way yourself, without the support of your soul, WITHOUT THE LINK."

For a moment my suffering is extreme, almost physical. Instantly I am overcome with vertigo, I do not feel the hot sun, nor how tired I am; I am just sad. I am separated from my real family, from myself. I move out into in the heat, walking in circles.

Quickly I pull myself together and discover another temple, a secret place, rarely visible to humans. It is the temple of Love/ Wisdom. Smaller than the pyramids, it is nonetheless striking in its strength and purity.

Entering the temple, I feel the shock of waves that are powerful, almost electrifying. Successions of white and blue vibrations surround me. On my 3rd eye, I bear the six-pointed star.

This symbol, its energy, penetrates my being and continues to remain there until the end of this initiation. My hands are free.

196

VOLUNTARILY, I REBUILD the bridge on the back of my neck and connect it to a secret spot in my body.

Immediately, white waves undulate around me, enter me. From the back of the temple there emerges a formidable, sweet presence, surrounded by the Light. She is the Mother, the Goddess, revealing herself to anoint me.

The Serpent, still within me, has completely mutated; he is Light. Suddenly I want to feel him more intensely, 'the way I used to.' I try to pull him up, to wake up the mechanism. But something unexpected occurs. On the sides of my first chakra, two spots begin vibrating. The first center is pulsating, open, clearly defined. Stubborn, I pull the energy up. It rises up abruptly, perfect, clear, strong and illuminates my pineal gland with Soma, three times. The pineal gland, the brain are on fire, my whole body is surrounded with Light, is Light: then I, all my tiny cells, receive a fabulous rejuvenating bath.

* * *

SECURITY SYSTEM

The Alta Major center located at the base of the skull, at the center of the nape and the top of the spine. Dormant in most individuals, it no longer plays its role as a key for the opening of the other chakras or as an antenna giving access to the spiritual realms. The area where the Alta Major is situated is a nervous and etherical crossroads; in fact, since the substance of which it is made is more subtle than nervous tissue, the term nadis would be more appropriate. Originally, there was a gland there, connected to what we now call the carotid.

We have been told that human DNA was reduced in order to en-slave humankind. In fact, the human race was modified in order to fully play its role in the scheme of the spiritual Hierarchies, and to participate in the karma of the planet and its Logos. The Alta Major is the center that was used to block human capacities.

Let's keep in mind that we are the body of the Logos, and that any action of the All in One, in the grandiose Universe, occurs in a timeless and matterless space. Whatever we, as humans, might consider good or bad, with our present awareness and judgmen-tal abilities, has nothing to do with the logic of the Creation and the evolution of the Universe. An event that creates change in the faculties of the creature or in its life might be momentarily felt as painful, but, in fact, it is beneficial.

Until the 3rd race, mankind had direct and easy contact with the spiritual realms. Because of this, the human was not perfectly incarnated. Man was closer to animal-man, because he did not have the seed of the mind. The fire of the mind was activated when the Sanat Kumara and his Hierarchy arrived on the planet. With the mind, intelligence replaced instinct; humans had to learn to differentiate. This means the ability to recognize the Self and non-self, to develop a sense of intuition and make choices be-tween good and bad, light and dark. In order for this to happen it was necessary to have access to the full range of frequencies, from Light to dark. The human race had to incarnate fully, to enter matter completely, without an easy access to the spiritual dimensions. This moment/passage in the evolution of humankind meant having to cut THE LINK BETWEEN HEAVEN AND EARTH, THE VERY LINK YOU NOW NEED TO REBUILD.

In the Tradition, this bridge is called Antakaranah. The rupture manifested itself on the etherical/physical plane, on the Alta Major. Human beings are connected with the Monad and the spiritual

kingdoms by spiritual 'threads'. The thread of life or Sutratma is the energy connection between the Divine Self and one's own personality. The three permanent atoms are like pearls hanging from the Sutratma, and they endure from one incarnation to the next; Sutratma vitalizes the Ego through the top of the head. From there, the energy is distributed through 3 centers:
- Pineal gland
- Pituitary gland
- Alta Major.

The next thread, called Antahkaranah, linking personality and Monad, has to be built by the Initiate in order to:
- Receive fully and consciously the impulse of the Monad.
- Integrate himself perfectly in the Hierarchy. In fact, the Antahkarana goes further in the body of the Logos and so on.

ALTA MAJOR, DEFINITION

The Alta Major, as well as the chakras, although it is non-physical, is nevertheless the link on the physical plane. It is the communication center, between the energy of life, flowing in Sutratma nadi, and the fires ascending along the spine and activating Kundalini.

The Alta Major is a KEY; it allows us to establish a close contact between the soul and the spiritual realms. It completes the system of the 7 etherical chakras, making possible the coordination and synergy of the centers. It is also the area where the bridge to the spiritual dimensions is to be built. Only after creating this bridge is the disciple capable of restoring a complete connection with his/her Monad. This means that instead of brief encounters with the God within, the student is in constant fusion with the Divine. From then on, the continuity of consciousness is possible. The activation of the Alta Major also promotes a faster opening up of the Lotus or Chalice. The latter, located above the head, is made up of 3 rows of petals, corresponding to the acquisition, by the student, of the frequencies of Knowledge, Love and Sacrifice.

For centuries the disciple who was building his chakras only developed the fourth center or Visuddha. But the throat chakra is the bridge between the body and the head. As such it opens up the path toward the three head centers that have to work in synergy. Visuddha is an intermediary because, when its energy is powerful enough and when the necessary frequency is reached by the student, Visuddha gives up its power to the Alta Major and to the upper triad (three upper chakras).

The fifth chakra then loses its importance and its energy is transferred to the Alta Major. The Alta Major then takes the main role in harmonizing the upper centers and the Total Self.

ROLE OF THE ALTA MAJOR

The Alta Major operates as an activator, a bridge, an extension of the Antahkarana.

The Alta Major, focal point of the human structure, functions in synergy with the pineal gland. Encompassing a crystal made of subtle energy, the Alta Major receives both the energies and the information provided by the spiritual planes. The crystal which is located in the Alta Major looks like a 10-pointed star and is linked with the ten systems that have contributed to the formation of the human creature. The blending of these systems was planned by the Infinite Consciousness in order to create a perfect being that would be the jewel of divine manifestation. This creature would have all of the most beautiful and most exceptional attributes already existing in the universe. The threads added to

200

the DNA are the results of these crossings or additions. The perfect human being is the manifestation of the might and the beauty of God's mind and Spirit.

When one activates and develops the faculties of the Alta Major, one triggers all the codes which have been seeded in human genetics throughout history. Also, because of the receptive quality of the crystal located inside the Alta Major, the blossoming of this center goes along with the unfolding of one's multi-dimensional consciousness.

The synergy with the pineal gland allows the integration and harmonization with the whole system or Consciousness that you are a part of. Thus, merging is possible between the human physical body and one's spiritual structure and Self, as well as integration of the specificities of neighbouring races and later of Spiritual realms.

When you focus your attention on the Alta Major, you are at once triggering and harmonizing all forms of your present life, blended with all your parallel existences, dimensions and inter-galactic codes. All are concentrated on one unique point. The crystal thus solicitated responds and registers any necessary information in the present. If the pineal gland is ready, the information will then be accessed by the brain. Then, when the merging with the pituitary occurs, one develops spiritual vision. And finally, when all these energy centers are merged with the throat chakra, you will manifest on the physical plane all that you have seen or perceived.

The Alta Major is also the anchor point of your multi-dimensional structure, called by some your Merkabah. The heart, too, is a point of connection but its role is different from the Alta Major.

RESULTS OF THE ACTIVATION OF THE ALTA MAJOR

At the physiological level, the awakening of Alta Major can be enhanced by astute application of the following methodologies:

Massage: Activation of all the glands, of the nervous systems, reduction of depression and tiredness. Balance of the sensations of thirst and hunger, bulimia. Balance of sleep.

Chiropractic torsion: Not recommended. Always adjust the sacrum prior to applying chiropractic force on the nape area.

Acupuncture: Release of all accumulated toxins. Freeing of one's psychic abilities. Clearing of memories and traumas pursuant to present and parallel lives. The needling or activation of the Alta Major restores communications with all ancestral frequencies encoded in the crystal. Do not needle irresponsibly, as many points in this area trigger headaches, dizziness and fatigue.
It is preferable to utilize energy and sound to open the Alta Major. Through toning, one activates one's codes with the intent of manifestation, i.e., in order to BE divine or to express God through spiritual duties and the daily routine. One's behavior and ability to reflect love and light are the best means to transmit the information encoded by the Masters of Light and by the Universe of Light, toward which humankind is moving.

The Alta Major is still not fully developed. In fact, it was atrophied. However, it is urgent that it be restored as quickly as possible so that it can be utilized as a chip, allowing telepathic communication and multi-dimensional transportation, and as a tool for manifestation. Toning of the Alta Major permits immediate manifestation.

During the creation of the universes, each race or category of creatures was encoded with different chips. Of course, these are not three-dimensional devices. The goal was not to enslave anyone, as chronic victims might think, but to have a way to call and wake up beings at the right time. In space, all information already exists within the matrix of matter, which is the receptive part of electricity. This information has to meet its complement/spiritual counterpart in order to be activated. When one learns how to create, one learns how to connect the elements through the activation of the vibrations of life. In order for a human on the path to be able to manifest, s/he must be in complete harmony with the frequency of life (no negative or suicidal thoughts allowed!). When one stands in harmony with Life and with the Whole, a mere thought or Presence brings/triggers the spark of communication or love.

The color blue is the closest to that of the Alta Major crystal. You can visualize the crystal turning on itself inside the center and beamed with blue light. This activation will automatically trigger a beam of energy to the pineal gland. Also through visualization, connect the Alta Major center with the soles of the feet, where Chinese point Kidney 1 is located. This point is found on the sole of the foot, in the hollow formed while crunching the toes. This technique enables clearing and restructuring of the energy of the adrenal glands as well as the ancestral energies, thus cleansing hereditary miasmas.

On the cabbalistic tree, the Alta Major is located on the central pillar at the cross-point of the rising energies. In most representations of the Tree of Life, there is a free space between Tiphereth and Kether called the Abyss. This is the gap that has to be crossed between the material and the divine worlds. Although some spiritual seekers have been able to cross the Abyss on their own through work, patience, endurance, and often tears, mankind as a group has been assisted in this task by the Spiritual Hierarchies.

In 1997, a comet crossed our system as the precursor of the Aquarian Era. The energy brought by Hale Bopp was a gift assisting mankind. The Sephiroth on the Tree of Life are planets that we could qualify as stable manifestations, although all creation is holographic in essence. A comet is a moving, non-fixed body, polarized differently. This explains the fascination exerted on humans by such phenomenon. The passage of the comet facilitated the end of the Hierarchy that was in charge at the time, and the transition toward the 4th dimension. Keep in mind that the Alta Major was the security system set into place by the Hierarchy which was responsible for the evolution of the planet. This spiritual government, under the authority of Sanat Kumara, forced the race to travel deep into matter and to forget Heaven momentarily in order to experience the opposite and learn to discriminate through the tool of the mind. This goal was reached. The race therefore started its ascending movement toward the reconquest of divinity. In fact, it is the remembrance of one's divinity that is available as soon as one integrates the Conscious Light or Light merged with the Darkness.

Daath, standing at the midpoint of the Abyss, is defined as such in the *Cabalistic Encyclopedia* by David Godwin: "Knowledge. Non-Sephirah, located in the Abyss below Chokmah and Binah but above Chesed and Geburah."

The Alta Major is the key, the link, in the physical body between Heaven and Earth, the invisible, spiritual spheres and the physical, visible ones. On the Cosmic plane, in the systemic body to which humankind belongs, the connection was established by a non-planet, by the Comet, which brought with it the vibration of the light and of the merging.

Hale Bopp, as witnessed by the chart of January 23rd 1997, carried the vibrations and the holographic image of the hexagram which, transposed in the fourth dimension, is the star tetrahedron.

Note: Planets, systems and galaxies are the bodies of Spiritual Beings and are thus under their responsibility. These gigantic consciousnesses are dedicated to the Divine Source and organized in Hierarchies, according to their personal evolution. The evolution of a planet or of a race is conducted by the Spiritual Hierarchies.

The student is encouraged to consciously re-activate the Alta Major and then reestablish connections between the chakras and the Alta Major. This is one of the fastest ways to attain alignment of the whole system and to raise up Kundalini.

Alignment is a stabilization of the forces that make up our triple being, physical, emotional and spiritual. To be able to reach this state, one has to work in two distinct and simultaneous ways:

1. Self-understanding and mastery of the personality.
Internal peace and balance are achieved in a very physical way through the alignment and the movement of the chakras in relation to one another.

2. Building up the bridges with mental/spiritual energy, using visualization techniques.

3. Alignment allows full communication and access to:
- the different parts of the Self
- other dimensions
- the Hierarchies, the planet, the solar system and so on.

PREPARATION TECHNIQUES:

BALANCING THE EMOTIONAL BODY

This technique is to facilitate the integration of your emotional body and its alignment with the physical and spiritual layers. It also reduces the turmoil and excesses associated with a lack of mastery of the emotions.

Located in the liver is the active essence of paternal heredity, written in the red blood cells. The spleen contains the maternal heritage, imprinted in the white cells. Father and mother are, of course, the symbols of the feminine and masculine energies, which must be balanced to achieve the raising up of Kundalini.

EXERCISE

- Assume a lotus position — or get as close to this position as you can.
- Breathe deeply, maintain a state of relaxation.

- Focus your attention on the **Ajna**. See the Light, possibly even the colors, that are associated with this center. When you are able to see/grasp this chakra correctly, connect it to two different spots in your body:
  • The **liver**, on your right side, with a golden bridge.
  • The **spleen**, on your left, with a silver link.

In essence, you are building a triangle whose apex is the Ajna. Stabilize this triangle of Light for 10 minutes.

ACTIVATION OF THE ALTA MAJOR:

- Sit between 3 candles.
- Visualize yourself surrounded by white Light, or imagine a column of Light originating from above your head and reaching down into the earth. You are in the center of the column.
- Ask for the presence of your guides or angels.
- Focus your attention on the nape, on a spot located in the center of the back of the neck, just under the skull.
- Imagine a ray of white Light entering this area, on the **Alta Major.**
- At the point where the Light is entering, visualize a blooming, opening flower.

Then, say these words out loud: "As a soul and a human being, I..., consciously reactivate my Alta Major, for a full connection with my spiritual selves, and the complete possession of my spiritual abilities."

OPENING OF THE CHANNELS OF ENERGY

It is advisable, during any period of intense growth, to maintain your spine in good condition. Ask for professional assistance if necessary. The progressive alignment of the energies generates a straightening of the bone structure. Conversely, severe pathologies or twisted vertebrae slow down the correct functioning of the energy system.

EXERCISE

- Be seated on a chair or in lotus position. Breathe deeply and relax.
- Visualize a ball of energy starting at the top of the head, making a stop in the nape and then going down to and back up all along the spinal column.
- Your intention, while you are visualizing, is to activate all the chakras.

Keep moving the energy up and down, several times, making a pause for several seconds at the root of each chakra.

ACTIVATING AND LINKING THE HEAD CHAKRAS

The following three techniques are preliminary to the specific and most important method using the Alta Major. You are to practice them for a period of at least 3 weeks, before using the "Alignment technique with the Alta Major'.

- In order to blend the soul with the personality, imagine a triangle of light, linking the **pineal** gland with your two **eyes**.

- To facilitate a clear and comprehensive vision of the facts, to understand events happening in the outside world as well as to increase your awareness of the scheme of the spiritual Hierarchy: connect the **forehead** chakra with the **eyes**.

HEAD CENTERS AND ALTA MAJOR

- Be seated in a lotus position, between 3 candles.
- Breathe deeply, relax, meditate.
- Stabilize yourself on the emotional triangle.
- When you feel centered, put your attention on the pineal gland and then stabilize yourself.
- Visualize a triangle of light between the **pineal**, the **pituitary** and the **Alta Major**.
- Finally, visualize bridges of light connecting the 5 areas mentioned above, i.e., **right eye, left eye, pineal, pituitary, Alta Major.**
- Do not spend more than 12 minutes a day in this position. Check whether or not you feel tired. Do not exert yourself in practicing this technique.
- Give thanks.

CONNECTION WITH THE HEART

- Assume a lotus position, breathe deeply, relax.
- Place your attention on the **center** of your **head,** where the pineal gland is located.
- When your attention is stabilized, bring to this area a globe of light that will activate the energy of this center.
- Then place your attention on the **throat** chakra, and, in the same way, activate it in bringing Light to it.
- Similarly, proceed with the **heart** chakra.

208

- Now, visualize **simultaneously** the luminous energy on the **three chakras, head, throat and heart.**

- When your vision/creation of this energy is completed and stable, visualize a triangle of Light that links together the 3 centers.

- Keep this image in your mind for ten minutes.

- Let go, take several deep breaths, give thanks.

ALIGNMENT WITH THE ALTA MAJOR

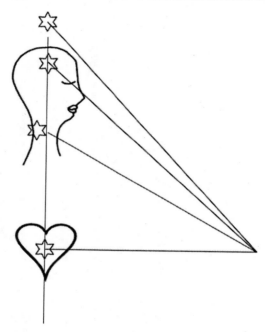

- Be comfortably seated, in the lotus position, or as close as possible, even if your posture is not perfect.

- Deep and slow abdominal breathing.

- Visualize a bridge, a ray of Light, linking up the **cardiac, throat, frontal** and **crown** chakras.

- When this link is created, visualize a spot in front of your body, about a foot ahead of the cardiac chakra. This dot will, of course, be made out of Light.

209

- Then, connect this **spot** successively with the **cardiac**, **throat**, **frontal** and **crown** centers, using rays of Light, and keeping the vertical bridge as previously established.

- Finally, trace bridges of Light, rays between this spot (in front of your heart) and:

> - The **Alta Major**, the **cardiac** chakra, the **spot**.
> - The **Alta Major**, the **throat** chakra, the **spot**.
> - The **Alta Major**, the **frontal** chakra, the **spot**.
> - The **Alta Major**, the **crown** chakra, the **spot**.

- Do not spend more than 12 minutes a day on this exercise.
- Give Thanks

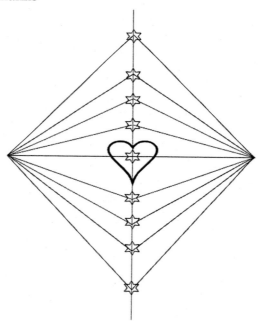

The previous technique is enough to make a good and fast jump in your personal growth. However, if you expend the alignment technique to the seven chakra system, you note the creation of a lozenge, and then, in three dimensions of an octahedron, the code and symbol for the harmonization of Spirit and Matter.

APPENDIX

INTRODUCTION TO SPIRITUAL HOMEOPATHY

MODIFY YOUR HEALTH
TO PURIFY YOUR FREQUENCIES

The healing process, the reintegration of the vital force begins with the mental mechanisms, and leads to a very personal change, one which is taking place on a cellular level, a change that is not only a remarkable metamorphosis of the intensity but also of the quality of your emanation.

In the past, this transmutation would occur very slowly. Today you have available to you a great deal of help. You are being bombarded by the vibrations of the planet and the planetary Logos, as well as by the vibrations of the spiritual Hierarchies and the Great White Brotherhood. You are also receiving a very specific influence from the evolving solar system, from powerful astrological transits, as well as frequencies broadcast by your extra-terrestrial neighbors. This inflow is helping you to remember easily and to become more open to awareness and knowledge.

Nevertheless, any new information, any frequency that touches your brain cells is just an opening, a beginning. Whatever information you have stored in your memory, it must be activated in order to become productive.

For instance, you might hear something about time travel or multi-dimensions. These terms will not make sense to you until the time when you actually feel them, in your cell's, in your own body. When that time comes, you will be able to say that you have understood and fully integrated this knowledge.

A new process, then, has been initiated on the physical level. The body has had access to areas of frequencies that until now have been neglected, laying dormant. Your intellect, in modifying itself, will change the quality of your thoughts, i.e. the vibratory flow in which you are living and evolving. Your physical envelope, in conjunction with your brain and spiritual body, is waking up. Your body is recalling its innate but unused natural abilities and is now allowing you to use them. As this happens, the physical vehicle will ask for help from external frequencies, vibrations of being. Little by little, your genetic code and DNA will renew itself.

Homeopathy gives both the body/mind information on how to modify its magnetic field. This type of medicine, then, is perfectly appropriate to complement the efforts made by the disciple.

ILLNESS, DEFINITION

Illness is a disintegration of the mental programming. Every thoughts that is positively oriented, will uplift you rather than humiliate you; in a very literal sense of the word, they will "built" you.

"Man is at the junction of intelligent active substance and of original will or Spirit. He is the child born of their marriage or coming into harmony." Alice Bailey. Treatise of Cosmic Fire.

The system of energies that you function in is based in duality, the marriage of positive and negative forces, white and black,

Yin and Yang. The challenge of the apprentice god is to discover these two polarities in himself, to experiment with and then balance them.

Before you reach this glorious state, you are subject to extreme sensations and experiences. Consciously or not, you ask for these challenges so that you can study the whole range of vibrations that make up the beauty of creation. Of course, you like exciting and sometimes very dangerous situations that might possibly lead you to a dead end. When this happens, you turn gloomy, lose yourself in sadness and depression. Your body follows your lead and, in turn, experiences stress and fatigue, before finally becoming ill.

During your terrestrial journey, it is not always possible to avoid problems or negative experiences. Nevertheless, you can always choose the way in which you react to outside events as well as challenges that you have created for yourself. How you respond will determinate not only your state of physical and emotional health, but also your - more or less - rapid progress toward a positive and favorable position.

Thus, when you find yourself in a difficult and negative situation, you have a stubborn tendency to harmonize yourself in a negative way instead of balancing the problem through sending out clear thoughts.

Positive energies build up; the entire chain of negative energies is an entropic system, leading to self-destruction. To wallow in an attitude or thoughts based on doubts, apprehension or sadness, is, in a way, to commune with the dark side of the universe. This also holds true for a lack of self-esteem, the inclination to see only the wrong side of things.

Illness sets in, then, when one's life or belief system is based on seeing things in an entropic vein rather than through creation. It is a destruction created but too heavy a pressure from the negative frequency. This vibration generates a reversal of the rotary movement of the chakras and produces a general weakening. Thus, it is important for each of us to pay attention to our mental state, our thoughts, our environment.

A negative state of mind might stem from a person's genetic inheritance, the "data" he came into incarnation with, related to his past/parallel lives. In this case, the vital force will be marked by these destructive inclinations. Work in self-discovery will be necessary, as well as deep cleansing, in order to bring about a change in the DNA structures.

These negative patterns also have their origin in childhood situations or in one's education. In fact, it is helpful to get rid of thoughts and their related patterns that stem from a model in the past; it is helpful to recreate the programs of your personality and arrive at a stabilized health. In-depth work on the subconscious mind will then modify parts of the vital force.

A deep healing of the subconscious mind will allow for a modification of certain aspects of the vital force. Finally, after a great deal of effort, the student will be ready to welcome Kundalini, who, while passing through the etherical channels, will purify the ganglions of the nerves, on both sides of the spine and change the individual's atomic structure. This does not mean of course, that the disciple will suddenly be in perfect health - but he will at least feel a noticeable improvement in his general state of being as well as a higher level of energy.

The key, then, is to accept and to love yourself, to appreciate the life you have chosen in order to nourish, within yourself, the Love-Creation vibration every single moment of your life.

Finally, the intensity, the health and integrity of your Vital Force depends upon your relationships, your interactions with the surroundings in which you are evolving, as well as the people with whom you associate.

Nothing is in a greater motion, more malleable, than energy. We are made up of energy, and because of our weaknesses, our mental and emotional instability, we are unusually subject to change. Thus we have a tendency to attract other beings whose frequency is a burden for us more than a source of strength. A good life style implies then frequenting places and associating with people who will nurture and honor us instead of draining us.

CHAKRA THERAPY
HOMEOPATHIC REMEDIES
THAT STIMULATE AND ATTUNE THE CHAKRAS:

The remedies listed below have not been tested according to the usual methods. But a number of them have been used with success. We can only suggest to health practitioners that they expend their concept of homeopathy.

Listed below are some suggested remedies :

1st chakra:
- Water element: Hydrophobinum
- Earth element: Natrun Muriaticum
- Fire element: Aurum Metallicum
- Air element: Tuberculinum, Natrum Sulfuricum, Phosphorus

If one is deliberately working on the kundalini: Naja X 1000, Lachesis X 1000, 3 times, one month apart, with:
- Abdominal breathing
- Grounding exercises
- Daily meditation
- Concentration on the 1st center, asking the Higher Self for assistance.

In this regard, we noticed in people interested in Kundalini arousal or practicing intensive yoga the signs of the snakes remedies.

2nd chakra: Hydrophobinum, Thuya.

3rd chakra: Bach nosodes, Nux Vomica, Lycopodium. Sulfur.

4th chakra: Gelsemium, Ignatia, Belladonna, Aurum Metallicum..
5th chakra: Mercurius Vivus et Solubilis. Lachesis. Ignatia.

6th chakra: Platina. Cobalt.

216

EQUINOX CEREMONY 1996

The main planetary moments in the year are, for the spiritual Hierarchy; the Solstice, Equinox, the Wesak ceremonies (full moon of May). On the Equinox, I contacted the Great White Lodge of Sirius.

The active members of the Great White Brotherhood are gathered in the room of "The Twelve". Standing up in a powerful, meditative circle, we strike up together the equinox chant. Rapidly the sounds are generating a dome of energy above us, whose apex is pointed toward the Galaxy.

Sanat Kumara appears, by himself, from the center of his total being, from four main rays, emerges a form, the imprint of a majestic and powerful face, reflection of his personality. Sanat Kumara blesses the room and his energy merges with the dome — sum of the vibrations of the Great White Brotherhoods members.
Sanat Kumara is now surrounded by the six other Kumaras, three on each side. The seven merge together as a unique body.

At this point, the 7 brothers position themselves as a line in order to welcome the 7 wives, the Pleiades. The marriage takes place according to a linear and crossed pattern. A complete inter-relation of the energies — male/female, 7 frequencies — is renewed for the month and year to come.

Then the intergalactic Princes and Lords of neighboring planets arrive from all the directions and introduce themselves to participate in the ongoing ceremony. A magnificent ballet is now occurring wrapped in the celestial colors and lights of the space and bathed in subtle music. According to the systemic scheme, the vibrations of the terrestrial and solar Hierarchies is building and organizing itself. In a sublime dance/meditation, the Kumaras and the Pleiades harmonize themselves with their galactic companions.

Each planetary energy is experienced individually and separately by the attendants, then implanted in our systems. We are infused by the blended energy of the galaxy, so that its pattern, its frequency, deeply imprinted in the Lodge may be redistributed.

Finally, the Kumaras stand, by themselves, in the center of the ceremony. They are now merging in order to form a unique ray, harmonized on the cardiac chakra. This Christic ray enters each member through his own cardiac center. Then, the ray succesively touches the soles of our feet, the palms, the throat, forehead. We are all vibrating in unison, nurturing ourselves with this conjugated power. Next, the ray clarifies our main chakras which begin to gleam and open themselves even more, as magnificent corollas. A serpentine, fire like energy, coils itself, merges with our glorious bodies.

The Kumaras leave, the Brothers bend over, on their knees and give thanks for the privilege and joy for participating in the work of the Hierarchy. Then, the members of the Great White Lodge position themselves so as to form an intricate precise pattern, based on the multiple of 12. This model will allow the attendants to scatter all over the planet and to broadcast the vibratory flux generated during the ceremony.

Notes

Notes

Notes

Notes